The distinction between Jewish and goyish can be quite subtle: Fidel Castro? Jewish, of course. Henry Kissinger—goyish. Marlon Brando—Jewish. Ringo is Jewish. Paul is goyish. George is goyish. John, of course, was Jewish.

EVERY GOY'S GUIDE TO COMMON JEWISH EXPRESSIONS

chicken soup
An ancient miracle drug...the only ailment it can't cure is neurotic dependence on one's mother.

no khoupie, no shtupie
The Jewish princess' equivalent to "no tickee, no washee."

EVERY GOY'S GUIDE TO COMMON JEWISH EXPRESSIONS

ARTHUR NAIMAN

ILLUSTRATED BY
RICK HACKNEY, JEFF LEEDY,
MARY ROSS AND GAR SMITH

BALLANTINE BOOKS • NEW YORK

Any similarity between the names used in jokes and the actual names of real people is completely unintentional and accidental, except for the names of friends of mine, who love the idea.

Thanks to Kitty Bruce for permission to quote extensively from Lenny Bruce.

Library of Congress Catalog Card Number: 81-6435

ISBN 0-345-30825-5

This edition published by arrangement with Houghton Mifflin Company

Manufactured in the United States of America

First Ballantine Books Edition: January 1983

ACKNOWLEDGMENTS

Without Harold Eiser's expertise to guide me, none of the Yiddish in this book would be correct. Since he was only able to look at part of the manuscript (and since I didn't always follow his advice), mistakes undoubtedly remain. Alan Levinson clarified many questions about Jewish culture. Suzy Locke did a superb job of networking.

None of these people saw the whole book, and there are numerous things in it that they probably won't like, so I want to very clearly and explicitly absolve them from any responsibility for, or agreement with, my point of view.

Cheryl Nichols and Vic Fischer gave me support in at least a dozen different ways. Their friendship made writing this book a much less difficult project than it would otherwise have been.

My agent, Michael Larsen, worked his ass off for me. In addition to having superb taste in manuscripts, Ellen Joseph is considerate and fair. Mike Harrison helped far, far beyond the call of duty. Tony Pietsch gambled on a stranger and we both won.

Special thanks to David Socholitzky and Sandy Van Broek of my Joke Supply Bureau. And a tip of the yamulka to Court Miller, who encouraged me to write funny stuff, read the manuscript at two different stages, and taught me how to body surf.

I also want to thank little Miss Arthur Naiman, without whose many long hours at the word processor this manuscript would have never been completed.

The following people did one or more of the following things—read a draft of the book; read a draft of the proposal; served as a member of my Panel of Distinguished Goyim; provided emotional support at 6 A.M. (and other times); lent me money; put great quantities of my deathless prose to death; stole Pentagon-Paper-esque amounts of photocopying for me; dressed up in funny costumes; drew funny pictures; told me about restaurants or words or jokes or species of African birds; advised me; made suggestions; and/or simply encouraged me (they also serve who only stand and kvell):

Rita Gibian, Bob Levy, Jim Mosher, Diane Sipes, Kareen Abdul Zuckerman (not her real name), Xenia Lisanevich (formerly Lila Dargahi—*both* real names), Alain Blondel, Anne Blondel, Marie Wilson, Lenore Friedman, Susan McCallister, Albert Naiman, Nettie Naiman, Sharon Sofia, Hope Winslow, Nancy Bovee, Helena Bentz, Janice Byer (ex-shicksa), Don Hadley, Matt Rinaldi, John O'Donnell, Angie Stone, Sakeena Spenčer, Val Stoller, Walter Maibaum, Ananda August, Janet Pfunder, Heidi Ellison, David Weidenfeld, Pippa Franks, Kaz Tsuchiya, Tak Tsuchiya, Paul Drexler, Kathy Reid, Sonya Blackman, Richard J. Lee, Pat Gigliotti—and especially Roz Kulick and Ron Lichty.

Any mistakes or inaccuracies in the text are, of course, entirely the responsibility of these people. For whatever virtues remain, I must accept full credit.

FOREWORD

High up in the castle, the dotted swiss curtains flutter in the wind, and the light of the full moon falls through the open window onto the flagstone floor of the princess's bedroom.

A sudden rustle at the window—a vampire has perched on the window sill. He slips down to the floor and creeps toward the princess in her bed. As his shadow falls across her face, she stirs in her sleep and opens her eyes.

Terror distorts her delicate features. She wrenches herself upright; one hand clutches her nightgown tight around her neck, the other snatches a silver crucifix from her bedside table. This she holds, trembling, between herself and the vampire's drooling fangs.

He looks at the crucifix, smiles, and says: "Sorry, lady, 'svet gornisht helfen."

You watch your friends as they laugh at this joke, their dark curls shaking. Once again you're on the outside looking in. A tear forms in the corner of your pale blue eye; it runs across your freckled cheek and drops to your forearm, where it nestles in the soft blond hair.

"Why wasn't I born Jewish!" a voice within you screams. But screams won't help. Screams can't make you pass for Jewish. Only this book can do that.

In its pages you'll find over 500 definitions of Jewish words and phrases, more than most Jews know themselves. With this book to help you, you would have known that "'svet gornisht helfen" means "it won't help a bit."

Pray as you might to your strange, well-groomed God, you can't turn back the clock and be born Jewish. But with this book, a little hair dye, and a nose job, you can be "born-again Jewish."

Mazel tov! (Look it up.)

INTRODUCTION

When I mentioned the idea for this book to friends, the typical response was: "that's a great idea, but hasn't it been done before?" Strangely enough, it hasn't. All previous books on the subject have either been of the total immersion, all-you-ever-wanted-to-know-about-Jewish-culture-and-more variety, or the thirty-four-cute-definitions-we'll-make-a-fast-buck-on-this-impulse-item variety.

Every Goy's Guide is a complete dictionary of every Jewish expression you're likely to come across in a conversation, joke, book or movie. But it doesn't talk to you as if you're thinking of converting, or make you wade through obscure details on (say) the most famous pseudo-messiah of seventeenth-century Turkey.

Every Goy's Guide contains hundreds of entries not found in *The Joys of Yiddish*. English as well as Yiddish expressions are included, as are the names and ingredients of Jewish dishes. Every definition includes a pronunciation, and many give examples of the word in use. Both the selection and the definitions are completely uncensored.

If you run across a word or phrase you think should be in here and isn't, drop me a line in care of Houghton Mifflin Company, Two Park Street, Boston, MA 02108. But I think you're going to have a hard time finding one.

In the meantime, enjoy the book. A tsadik it won't make you, but at least it will keep you from being a nar.

SPELLING AND PRONUNCIATION

Schmuck looks funny without the first **c** (and even funnier without the second), and it takes a lot of chutzpah to spell **chutzpah** "khootspuh." So wherever certain spellings have come to be accepted as more or less standard renditions of Jewish words in English, I've used them. (Trying to make English spellings phonetic is a hopeless task anyway.)

I've cross-indexed variant spellings and have included pronunciations for each word, except those that sound exactly the way they're spelled.

Contrary to what you may have heard, Yiddish isn't hard to pronounce. The only sound it uses that isn't found in English is **kh,** which is pronounced like the **ch** in the German *achtung* or the Scottish *loch*.

Of course there's also **kv,** but saying that right is just a matter of believing you're actually supposed to say **k** and then **v** without putting a vowel between them. (The same goes for **kn.**)

Ts doesn't occur at the beginning of words in English as it does in Yiddish, but the sound itself is exactly the same as at the end of *cuts,* or *shuts* (not to mention *putz*).

KEY TO PRONUNCIATIONS

As much as possible, I've tried in the pronunciations to use spellings that can only be pronounced one way, or at least are very commonly pronounced one way.

a as in has
ah as in shah
aw as in saw
ay as in say
e or **eh** like the **e** in met
ee as in bee
ei as in height
i as in hit
o or **oh** like the **o** in no
oo as in zoo
ŏŏ as in took, could, put
   This is a very common sound in Yiddish and should never be mispronounced **oo** or **uh,** as in *boobie* or *buhbie*
ow as in cow
u or **uh** like the **u** in but
ch always as in Charlie
g always as in get
kh—as mentioned above, like the **ch** in the German *ach* or the Scottish *loch*
s always as in last
z always as in haze
zh always like the **z** in azure

Stressed syllables are written in capital letters. Words of one syllable are written in lowercase, because they're easier to read that way. When the syllables of longer words each receive equal stress, they're written all in lowercase too.

ADJECTIVE ENDINGS

Strictly, Yiddish adjectives have three kinds of endings: **uh** (which I spell **-a**)—for feminine and plural nouns; **er** (masculine); and no ending (neuter). But most American Jews use only two: **uh** and no ending (**fleishedika, fleishedik; goyisha, goyish**).

Many adjectives have only one form (for example, **fershimilt,** never **fershimilta**). When both endings exist, their use depends not on gender, but on position in the sentence: **uh** is normally used when the adjective comes before a noun ("What a **fercockta** distinction!"), and dropped when the adjective stands alone ("this distinction is **fercockt!**"), although the **uh** ending is sometimes used there too.

CROSS-REFERENCES

(qv) after a word (or words) means it's got a definition of its own and that you'll find more information on the subject you're reading about if you read that definition too. (**qv** stands for *quod vide,* by the way, which is Latin for "which [you should] see.")

DEFINITIONS

A

a bi gezunt (ah BEE guh-ZŎONT)

So long as you're healthy.

This expression does *not* mean "Be healthy!" or "Good health to you!" It means, "Don't worry so much about that problem, whatever it is. You've still got the most important thing, your health." *Fired, shmired, a bi gezunt.*

Sometimes a bi gezunt is used ironically, as in the classic *cancer, shmancer, a bi gezunt.*

(Also see **gezunt, gay gezunt, tsu gezunt** and **zei gezunt.**)

accent (Jewish)

I just put this entry in so I could tell you this joke:

My aunt Rita had just arrived in Hawaii for the first time. On her way to get her baggage, she passed a gray-haired man selling newspapers. "Excuse me," she said, "I've always wondered: what's the correct way to say the name of your state? Is it Hawaii or Havaii?"

"Havaii," the man said.

"Thank you."

"You're velcome."

adonoy (ah-do-NOY)

A name for God, usually translated "Lord."

You're only supposed to use the word adonoy in prayer, and pious Jews substitute the word **adoshem** outside of shul. But even adonoy is a euphemism.

The *real* name of God is composed of the four letters YHVH (sometimes incorrectly transliterated as JHVH) with some set of vowels between them (as in JeHoVaH, but "juh-HO-vuh" isn't necessarily the right pronunciation). I once got a devout housemate very upset by playing around with all the possible combinations of vowels, hoping to hit on the right one (along the lines of Arthur C. Clarke's "The Nine Billion Names of God"—except, of course, there aren't nine billion ways to pronounce YHVH).

The idea is that the *real* name of God is so holy it should never be spoken aloud, even in prayer. This is similar to the belief of many primitive peoples who distinguish between the name by which everyone knows a person and that person's "true" name. Anyone who learns your true name has you in their power. So you can see why God wants to keep her true name secret. (A wonderful story on this theme is Ursula Le Guin's "The Rule of Names.")

(Also see **golem**.)

afikomen (ah-fee-KO-mun)

A piece of matza hidden by the adults before the Passover seder begins.

In the middle of the meal, when the kids are getting restless, they're sent to look for the afikomen. The one who finds it gets a small prize of some kind. This provides a nice change of pace from listening to the Haggadah and stuffing your face.

In some families, the kids hide the afikomen themselves after they find it. Then they hold it for ransom and only return it when the adults give them the prize.

(Afikomen comes from the Greek word for "dessert.")

a gezunt af... or **an...** (see **gezunt**)

a guter mensch nor der bayzer hunt lost nisht tsu tsu

im (ah GŎOT-er MENSH nawr dayr BAY-zer HŎONT LAWST nisht tsoo tsoo EEM)

A good man, but his mad dog won't let you near him. (If only you could get past his assistant, wife, secretary, chief counselor, bodyguard or whoever. . . .)

A.K. (see **alter cocker**)

a kham mit bildung iz nisht mer vie a gebilditer kham (ah KHAHM mit BIL-dŏong iz NISHT MAYR vee ah guh-BILD-it-ayr KHAHM)

A boor with education is still just an educated boor.

a khesorun, die kala iz tsu shayn! (ah kheh-SAWR-un, dee KAH-luh iz TSOO SHAYN)

The problem is, the bride is too pretty. (By you, *this* is a *problem?*)

Used when someone seems to be looking everywhere to find excuses to avoid accepting a situation.

-ala (uh-luh)

This diminutive can be translated as "little" or "my little." For example, *And where is Suzala?* means "And where is my little Susan?"

The affection can be further intensified by saying something like: *And where is my little Suzala?* which means: "And where is my darling, cute, little Susan?"

This can be *further* intensified by saying something like: *And where is my darling, cute, little Suzala?* and so on *ad nauseam*.

This ending also occurs as **-ul** (uhl), as in **boychikul** (qv).

aleichem shalom (uh-LAY-khim shuh-LOM)

And to you, peace. The response to **shalom aleichem** (qv).

alle yevonim hoben ayn ponim (AH-luh yuh-VAWN-im HAH-bin AYN PAW-nim)

All brutes have the same face; all cruel, insensitive people look alike.

The Hebrew word *yevanim*—singular: **yoven** (YAW-vin)—meant "Greeks," whom the Hebrews considered amoral and barbaric. In later times yevonim came to mean any brutal people, like the Cossacks and Russian soldiers who instigated pogroms.

Traditionally, Jews have responded to yevonim with wit rather than force, as was the case with the Jew who accidentally bumped against one on the sidewalk.

"Swine!" snarled the yoven.

The Jew bowed and said, "Horwitz."

(Also see **vie a yoven in suka.**)

alter cocker (AHL-ter KAHK-er)

An old fart; a derogatory way to refer to an old man. (Literally, "old shitter.")

Abbreviation: **A.K.** (I just prefer to spell it with a **c**, that's all. I don't have to have a reason.)

an einredenish iz erger vie a krenk (ahn EIN-red-en-ish iz AYR-gayr vee ah KRAYNK)

A delusion is worse than a sickness.

Ashkenazim; adjective: **Ashkenazic** (ahsh-ken-AHZ-im or -eem; ahsh-ken-AHZ-ik)

Jews from central or eastern Europe, as opposed to Sephardim—Jews from Spain, Portugal, North Africa and other Mediterranean countries. The overwhelming majority of American Jews (and of all Jews worldwide) are Ashkenazim.

In his book *The Thirteenth Tribe,* Arthur Koestler argues that there weren't enough Sephardic Jews in all of western and southern Europe to account for the sudden population explosion of Jews in Eastern Europe in the late Middle Ages, and that they therefore had to have come from somewhere else. He makes a very convincing case for the theory that the Ashkenazim are descendants of a Turkish nation called the Khazars who converted to Judaism *en masse* around 750 A.D., when their power and prestige required that they replace their tribal religion with a major, monotheistic one.

Apparently they picked Judaism to avoid having to choose between the religions of their two major rivals: Christian Byzantium and the Islamic Caliphate of Baghdad. As Jews, they could maintain their neutrality, or at least switch allies freely.

From around 950–1500 A.D. the Khazars were driven westward by successive invaders; they were particularly devastated by the Golden Horde. Many of them ended up in Poland and Lithuania, where they dealt extensively with non-Jewish German traders and developed a *lingua franca* based on German, with many words borrowed from Hebrew and Slavic tongues. This language (Yiddish) gradually replaced the original Khazar tongue (much as English has replaced Yiddish for most American Jews), except in the case of fundamentalist Ashkenazic sects like the Karaites, who still speak a Turkic dialect.

If Koestler is right, Ashkenazim would be properly defined as "Jews descended from the Khazars" and only Sephardim could claim to be descended, even remotely, from the Hebrews.

(Ashkenaz was originally a Hebrew name for an ancient kingdom in eastern Armenia. In medieval rabbinical usage, it became a name for Germany.)

az an oriman est a hun, iz oder er krank oder die hun (ahz ahn AWR-uh-mahn est ah HŎON, is AW-dayr AYR KRAHNK AW-dayr dee HŎON)

When a poor man gets to eat a chicken, it's either because he's sick . . . or because the chicken is.

az an oriman est a hun, iz oder er krank oder die hun

az gott zol voynen af der erd, volten die menschen bei im die fenster oysgeshlogen (ahz GAWT zawl VOY-nen ahf dayr AYRD, VAWL-ten dee MENSH-en bei eem dee FEN-ster OYS-ge-shlaw-gen)

If God lived on earth, people would break his windows.

az me fregt die sheila, iz trayf (ahz meh FREGT dee SHEI-luh, iz TRAYF)

If you ask them, they'll say you can't do it. (But if you *don't* ask . . .)

(This expression is a good example of how Yiddish mixes words with German and Hebrew origins. It's made up of: *as man fragt die*, "if one asks the" [German]; *sheila*, "question" [Hebrew]; *ist*, "[it] is" [German]; *trayf*, "not kosher" [Yiddish, from a Hebrew word].)

8

az me hot gelt iz men i klug, i shayn, i men ken gut zingen (ahz me HAWT GELT iz men ee KLŎOG, ee SHAYN, ee men ken gŏot ZING-un)

If you have money, you're intelligent, good-looking, and you're a good singer too.

(But you're not necessarily any fun to live with.) Here's a joke about that:

At an elegant charity affair, all the ladies are clustered around Mrs. Fishbein, who is wearing a truly enormous diamond.

"Yes," she tells them, "this is the fifth largest diamond in the world. It's called, of course, the Fishbein."

"Oh, how lucky you are!"

"Superficially I know it must seem that way. But unfortunately, with the Fishbein diamond there also comes the Fishbein curse!"

"What's the Fishbein curse?"

"Fishbein."

az me ken nisht beisen, zol men nisht sh'chiren mit die tsayn (ahz meh ken nisht BEI-sin, zol men nisht SH'CHEER-in mit dee TSAYN)

If you can't bite, don't growl (literally, . . . don't grind your teeth).

az me vawlt zikh gekent aroyskoyfen fun toyt, vawlten die orima leit a shayna parnossa gehat (ahz meh vawlt zikh guh-KENT uh-ROYS-koy-fun fawn TOYT, VAWLT-un dee AWR-ee-muh leit ah SHAYN-uh pahr-NAWS-uh guh-HAHT)

If people could hire people to die for them, the poor would make a nice living.

B

babka (BAHB-kuh)

A Russian/Polish coffee cake, which comes in several varieties.

bagel (BAY-gul)

A hard, doughnut-shaped roll, boiled and then baked.

I hope you're not depending on this definition to learn what a bagel is. If you've never had one, try your first toasted, with butter melted into it. The classic thing is to put cream cheese and lox (smoked salmon) on it.

As with anything, there are bagels and then there are *bagels*. So beware of bad imitations.

balabusta (bahl-uh-BŎOS- or -BAWS- or -BUS-tuh)

A bossy woman.

Also (and originally) the kind of housewife who keeps things so clean that you can "eat off her floor."

bar mitzvah (bahr MITZ-vuh)

The ceremony, held in a temple or synagog, in which a Jewish boy "becomes a man" at the age of thirteen.

He shows his worthiness by reading a few lines in Hebrew from the Torah, and gets lots of gifts.

In the ceremony, the boy declares, "Today I am a man." When I was bar mitzvahed, fountain pens were such common presents that there was a joke about the boy who got confused and declared, "Today I am a fountain pen."

"Bar mitzvah" literally means "inheritor of the commandment." The measure of an adult is the ability to understand the law (and the 613 duties—mitzvahs—it commands) well enough to perform them. Since children can't understand what God requires, they aren't required to do mitzvahs.

The bar mitzvah ceremony marks the point at which a boy can read and understand the law, and thus becomes responsible for following it. He now counts toward a minyan (qv) and, in the old days, was considered old enough to marry.

(Also see **mitzvah.**)

baruch ato adonoy (see **brawkha**)

bas mitzvah (bahs MITZ-vuh)

A bar mitzvah for a girl (at the age of twelve or thirteen—the practice varies).

Unfortunately, the commandment she's being dutiful to was never intended to be applied to women. In Orthodox shuls, women sit in a separate (and not equal) section. An ancient Jewish prayer goes: "Thank God I was not born a woman!" Obviously, the Bas Mitzvah is a twentieth-century invention.

batamt, batamta (buh-TAHMPT, -TAHMPT-uh)

Delicious, tasty.

bei mir bist du shayn (bei MEER bist doo SHAYN)

To me, you're beautiful—the title of a very popular song written by Sholem Secunda of the Yiddish theater. Made famous by the Andrews Sisters.

(Also see **by me.**)

bialy (bee-AHL-ee)

A flat, crusty roll with pieces of onion in a round depression.

Kossar's on Grand between Essex and Norfolk (on New York's Lower East Side), makes the best I've had.

(Bialy is short for *bialystoker pletsel,* "flat roll from Bialystok" (Poland), the town where it was presumably invented.)

bissel, bissela (BIS-ul, -ul-uh)

A little.

blintz (blints)

A wonderful dish, made of a pancake wrapped around a filling and fried. The filling is usually a dry, uncreamed cottage cheese (like ricotta), but fruit jam and other fillings are also used. (Put sour cream on your blintzes or—if the filling is cheese—jelly.)

If you don't want to try bagels, OK, fine, don't try them. But never to have eaten a blintz makes it pretty clear you have a goyisha kup.

(From the Ukrainian word for "pancake.")

B'nai Brith (buh-NAY BRITH)

A Jewish fraternal and charitable organization founded in 1843. Its Anti-Defamation League fights religious and racial prejudice, and its Hillel Foundation promotes Jewish culture on college campuses.

(The name is a Sephardic pronunciation of a Hebrew phrase meaning "sons of the covenant.")

bobkes (see **bupkes**)

bokher, bocher (BAW-kher)

Young man. Most often used in the phrase **yeshiva bokher** (qv).

boo boo
   1. A mistake.
   2. A minor wound.
   (Jerry Lewis brought this word, which comes from the Polish *bulba*—"potato"—into common usage.)

bopkes (see **bupkes**)

borsht (bawrsht)
   Orginally, any hearty peasant soup made with the cow parsnip (called *borshch* in Russian). Among American Jews, however, borsht almost always refers to a beet soup served hot or cold with sour cream, chunks of boiled potato, diced cucumbers, onions or pieces of hardboiled egg.
   There is, however, also cabbage borsht, made with meat, tomatoes, etc. For what is sometimes called spinach borsht, see **shchav.**

borsht belt (bawrsht belt)
   A group of Jewish resorts in the Catskill Mountains of New York State (Grossinger's, the Nevele, the Concord, etc.) where many famous comics got their starts, often working as tummlers (qv).

boubala (BŎO-buh-luh)
   An affectionate form of boubie, often used to address children, friends and lovers. *Oy, boubala, boubala—what's the matter now?*

boubameisa (BŎO- or BAH-buh-mai-suh)
   An old wives' tale; any superstition or unbelievable story.
   (From *bouba*, "grandmother" + Hebrew: *ma'aseh*, story.)

boubie, bouba (BŎO-bee, BŎO-buh)
   Originally—and still—"grandmother," but much more

13

frequently used as a casual term of affection between people, along the lines of "darling" or "sweetheart" or "baby." *Hey, boubie, how's it going?*

The classic boubie joke goes like this:

Yetta Socholitzky is lying on her deathbed. By her side are her two loving grandsons, Nate and Dave, owners of Nate and Dave's Discount Furniture. Yetta is fading fast, but she manages to say, "Nate, you here?"

"Yes, bouba."

"Dave? You here?"

"Yes, bouba."

With her last breath, Yetta gasps, "That's no good. Who's minding the store?"

To give you an idea of what a crucial role humor plays in the emotional life of many Jews, Nat Boonin tells me of a woman who actually went through that routine with her two sons on her own deathbed. To make a joke as you lie dying—I think that's pretty impressive.

(Boubie comes from the Slavic *baba*, "grandmother," which is commonly used to address any old woman.)

boychik, boychikul (BOY-chik, BOY-chik-uhl)

Little boy, darling little boy. *Boychikul* is more affectionate.

(Also see **-chik** and **-ala**.)

brawkha (BRAW-khuh)

A blessing, or prayer of thanksgiving.

Orthodox Jews "make a brawkha" at least 100 times a day—before eating or drinking anything (there are different brawkhas for different kinds of food), when they wash their hands, the first time they put on a new piece of clothing, when they smell a fragrant odor, or see the new moon, or lightning, a sunset, beautiful scenery, etc., etc.

Brawkhas often start with the words *baruch ato adonoy, eloheynu melech ho-olom*...(bah-ROŎKH ah-TAW ah-doh-

14

NOY, el-o-HAY-noo MEL-ekh haw-aw-LOM)—"blessed art Thou, oh Lord our God, King of the universe."

To this beginning specifics are added. For example:... *ha-motsi lechem min ho-orets* (hah-MO-tsee LE-khem min hah-AWR-ets)—"who bringest forth bread from the earth" (the prayer over the bread) or... *boray pree ha-gofen* (baw-RAY PREE hah-GAW-fun)—"who givest us the fruit of the vine" (the prayer over the wine).

briss

The ceremony at which eight-day-old Jewish boys are circumcised by a moyl (qv).

(From the Hebrew word for covenant.)

broche (see brawkha)

bubele (see boubala)

bubie (see bouba)

bubkes (see bupkes)

buhayma (buh-HAY-muh)

Literally, an animal, especially a cow. But mostly used to describe people who resemble animals by being stupid: *What does that buhayma know about anything?* or by being hard-working and uncomplaining: *He works like a buhayma from dawn to dusk.*

(From the Hebrew *behama*, "domesticated animal.")

buhaymisha (buh-HAY-mish-uh)

Animallike; dull.

bulvan (bŏol-VAHN)

A big bruiser; a lout.

bupkes, bopkes, bubkes, bobkes (BŎOP-, BAHP-, BAWP-, BŎOB-, BAHB-, BAWB-kess or -kiss. Sorry, but I've heard every one of these variations.)

An inadequate reward; peanuts (in the sense of something trivial).

Thirty years he worked for that momzer, slaving his fingers to the bone, and what does he have to show for it? ...bupkes!

Bupkes is Russian for "beans," but its figurative meaning probably comes from another sense of the word: goat or rabbit turds (which look like beans).

by me

In my opinion; in my experience. *By me, this is everything a fruit can be.*

Also **by you, by her** and so forth, as in *how's by you?*—"how are you doing?"

(Also see **bei mir bist du shayn.**)

C

cantor (CAN-tur)

A religious functionary who sings parts of the services in shul.

Any member of the congregation who has a good voice can be the cantor. Even the rabbi can be a cantor (which saves money). The Yiddish word for cantor is **khazen.**

CH

If you don't find a word you're looking for under CH, also check under **H** and **KH.**

chachka, chachkie, tsatska, tsatski (CHAHCH-kuh, CHAHCH-kee, TSAHTS-kuh, TSAHTS-kee)

A trinket, gadget, knick-knack or little toy. *A fly-blown little chachka stand on the Santa Monica pier* (Chandler).

Almost anything can be a chachka if it's small and not worth much money—porcelain statuettes, political buttons, cheap pieces of jewelry, wind-up toys, etc. The original meaning is "a child's toy."

The word can also be applied to any small thing that gives the cluttered appearance of chachkas; for example, a dress covered with tassels might be referred to as *the shmata with the chachkas all over it.*

Chachkala or **tsatskala** (CHACH-kuh-luh, TSATS-kuh-luh) is a diminutive often used as an affectionate way to address a child or a lover, more or less equivalent to "sweetie."

A chachka can also be a bruise or minor wound. *Where did you get that chachka on your arm—roughhousing with those goyim?!*

Another meaning for chachka (and particularly for chachkala) is an attractive young woman, seen primarily (or only) as a sex object. *Who was that little chachkala I saw Morris with last night?* This meaning is somewhat dated (as a word as well as a concept).

challah (KHAH-luh)
A braided egg bread, very light and delicate. Used particularly on the sabbath. Should be pulled off in pieces and eaten plain, not sliced (except for sandwiches).
(From the Hebrew.)

Chanukah (commonly: HAH-nuh-kuh; correctly: KHAH-nuh-kuh)
Jewish Christmas.

It's true—Chanukah was just a minor holiday whose importance grew enormously because it happens to fall at the same time as Christmas. But it couldn't have happened to a nicer holiday.

Chanukah celebrates the struggle of the Hebrew people to free themselves from Syrian domination in the second century B.C. They were led by a priest named Mattathias and his son Judah, who called himself Maccabee (the hammer). Poorly equipped and incredibly outnumbered, the Maccabean guerrillas nevertheless smashed the Syrians at Emmaus.

It's great to have a holiday that celebrates a fight against oppression, instead of some religious mumbo-jumbo. Unfortunately, not content to leave Chanukah political, the rabbis added some cockamamie story about how when the Great Temple in Jerusalem (wrecked by the Syrians) was rebuilt, one day's supply of oil miraculously lasted eight days. I think it's more miraculous when a bunch of ragtag guerrillas defeat a huge empire—whether in ancient Judea, or elsewhere.

Chanukah lasts eight nights, and on each night one more candle is lit on a special candleholder called a menorah (qv). You get presents on all eight nights. This alone makes Chanukah an improvement on—rather than just a substitute for—Christmas.

Chassid; plural: Chassidim or Chassids; adjective: Chassidic (KHAH-sid, khah-SEED-im, KHAH-sidz, khah-SID-ik)

The Chassidic movement began in the 1700s in central and eastern Europe as a sort of evangelical reaction against the traditional rabbinical emphasis on study and debate of the Talmud. The Chassidim danced, sang and prayed in the open, saying that God requires no synagogs except in the heart.

Chassids see their rabbis much more as charismatic leaders than other Jews do. A current Chassidic leader is the Lubavitcher Rebbe (i.e., the rabbi from Lubavitch).

However progressive the Chassidim may have been when they started out, they are now much more traditional than the average Jew. The men dress all in black and let their beards and **payess** (qv) grow. Married women keep their heads shaved and wear wigs. Of course these are things that all Orthodox Jews used to do, but there aren't many devout Orthodox Jews around anymore, other than the Chassidim.

There's a wonderful joke about the Chassid who goes to visit a distant cousin in Atlanta. As he gets off the train—with his broad-brimmed black hat, his long black overcoat, his thick red beard, and his payess flying in the wind—every head on the platform snaps around to stare at him. He endures this for a moment and then says, "Vat's de medeh? You never seen a Yenkee before?"

(From a Hebrew word meaning "pious.")

chazer (KHAHZ-ur)

Pig, both literally—the animal whose delicious, juicy flesh Jews are forbidden to eat—and figuratively—someone who is selfish, or who eats a lot.

chazerei (khahz-ur-EI)

Junk, worthless stuff; especially junk food. (Literally, "pig stuff.")

The word chazerei always brings to my mind those greasy orange-colored cheese puffs—Cheese Doodles, I think they're called. *What are you eating that chazerei for? Here, have a piece of fruit.*

chazerei

cheder (KHAY-dur)

Hebrew school.

Imagine, after spending all day locked up in public school, having to spend two or three more hours puzzling over funny-looking letters that go the wrong way across the page.

Only the lure of a bar mitzvah (in order to be bar mitzvahed, you have to read ten lines of Torah in the original Hebrew (or Aramaic, or whatever it is) (although of course you only learn how to sound out your particular passage, not to really understand the language (I'm talking about Reform Hebrew school here, not Conservative or Orthodox ("cheder" really means Orthodox Hebrew school—otherwise you just call it Hebrew school) because in Orthodox cheder, you really learn a lot (although of course there's a lot you *don't* learn, like how to fade when you make a jump shot, or what rubbers look like (you still with me here? let me go back and count up those parentheses...OK)))))—only the lure of your bar mitzvah, I say, where everyone will kvell over you and give you presents, sustains you during those long, dreary afternoons. By the time you leave, it's dark out— too late to play football, too late to do anything except go home and have dinner, watch some TV and go to bed, with nothing more to look forward to than another day of the same horrible grind. *Oy, 'siz shver tsu zein a yid!*

Actually, to be perfectly honest with you, I *asked* to go to Hebrew school and I kind of liked it. If you want a description of a really horrible cheder, read Henry Roth's *Call It Sleep* (a book with many other virtues to recommend it).

Chelm (khelm)

An imaginary town full of morons, the butt of innumerable jokes. I will restrict myself to one:

The rabbi from Chelm goes on a trip to Pinsk. Since he's from Chelm, the rabbi from Pinsk naturally doesn't want to waste his time on him, but the rabbi from Chelm is able to strike up a conversation with the shamus (caretaker).

After an exchange of pleasantries, the shamus asks him if he would like to hear a riddle.

"Of course. I love riddles."

"All right now, listen very carefully. This is tricky. Who is my mother's son, but not my brother?"

Well, the rabbi from Chelm is dumbfounded. Who could be this man's mother's son and not be his brother? No matter how he turns it around in his mind, he can't find an answer to the riddle. So at last he says:

"I give up. This is truly a difficult riddle. Who is your mother's son, but not your brother?"

"I am!" says the shamus from Pinsk gleefully.

Well, the rabbi from Chelm is dumbfounded a second time. That such cleverness could exist on the face of the earth! He can barely wait to get back to Chelm to tell everyone this extraordinary riddle.

On his return, he gathers all of Chelm in the town square and asks them: "Who is my mother's son, but not my brother?"

Well, needless to say, if the *rabbi* from Chelm can't figure out a riddle, there's not much chance anyone else in the town will be able to. They have trouble with questions like "what time is it?" Nevertheless, they make a valiant effort—stroking their beards, scratching their heads, pacing back and forth across the square. But of course it's all to no avail.

Finally the mayor, acting as their spokesman, says, "It's no use. We'll never figure it out. Tell us, rabbi: who is your mother's son, but not your brother?"

With a condescending smile, the rabbi answers: "The shamus from Pinsk, of course."

chicken soup

An ancient miracle drug containing equal parts of aureomycin, cocaine, interferon and TLC. The only ailment chicken soup can't cure is neurotic dependence on one's mother.

chicken soup

-chik

A diminutive ending, which can be translated as "little."
E.g. *boychik.*

-chikul

An even more diminutive ending, which can be translated
"darling little." E.g. *boychikul.*

choleria (khah-LAYR-ee-uh)

A plague, a disease, as in the expressions *zol dir chapn
a choleria* (zawl deer KHAH-pun uh khah-LAYR-ee-uh)
(may a disease catch you) or simply *a choleria* (on you).
   (Literally, "cholera.")

chometz (see **khometz**)

chopped liver (CHAHPT LIV—wait a minute. You know
how to pronounce this)

23

A completely wonderful dish if done right (which it rarely is). It must be made with chicken liver, not beef liver, and it must have enough onions; good chopped liver should be crunchy. **Gribbenes** (qv) are an essential ingredient.

chumesh (see **khoumish**)

chuppah (see **khoupa**)

chutzpah (KHŎOTS-puh)
Incredible gall; brazen effrontery. The classic example of chutzpah is the man who kills his mother and father and then asks the court for mercy because he's an orphan.

Here's the ultimate chutzpah joke:

A woman is walking along the beach with her young son in the dead of winter. She's lost in her own thoughts and doesn't notice that he has wandered too close to the water. Suddenly a giant wave comes crashing in and washes the boy out to sea.

A man walking nearby sees this happen. Without a moment's hesitation he tears his clothes off and plunges into the water. Jagged chunks of ice fly all around him but he swims steadily out into the freezing ocean. He reaches the boy just as he's going under for the last time.

Swimming back in, the man has to fight a strong undertow. Finally he staggers back onto the beach, only to discover that the boy has turned blue and isn't breathing. He lays him down on the sand and begins artificial respiration. Ten minutes, twenty minutes, half an hour go by, and still it's only the man's breath in the boy's lungs that's keeping him alive. At last the boy's eyelids flutter and he begins to breathe by himself.

Completely exhausted, half-dead from exposure, the man collapses next to the boy. Huge shudders rack his body; his breath comes in long, ragged gasps.

The boy's mother walks over and looks at her son, then turns to the man and says, "He *had* a *hat!*"

clop (see **klop**)

cockamamie (KAHK-uh-may-mee)
Half-assed, ridiculous, implausible. *He gave me some cockamamie excuse, but I know he was out with his chicken* (Lenny Bruce).

(Apparently a distortion of the word "decalcomania" by children in New York around the turn of the century. The idea is, if you put a decal on your arm, it's not a real tattoo, it's a cockamamie tattoo. By analogy, a half-assed excuse came to be called a cockamamie excuse. This is not strictly a Jewish word, but I've included it because much of its popularity comes from its use by Jewish comedians.)

cocked up (kahkt up)
Literally, "shitted up," but "fucked up" is a closer English equivalent.

cocker (KAHK-ur)
A term of disrespect. Most commonly used with "little"—*why you little cocker!*—or in the phrase **alter cocker,** "old fart." (Literally, "shitter.")

Conservative
Reform is the most liberal of the three Jewish religious denominations; Orthodox is the most traditional. Conservative is in between. (See **Reform** for more on the distinction.)

crypto-Jewish names
There are some goyisha names that just about guarantee someone isn't Jewish. For example, you'll never meet a

Jew named Johnson or Wright or Jones or Sinclair or Ricks or Stevenson or Reid or Larsen or Jenks. But some goyisha names just about guarantee that every other person you meet with that name will be Jewish. Why is this?

Who knows? Learned rabbis have pondered this question for centuries and have failed to come up with an answer, and you think *you* can find one? Get serious. You don't even understand why it's forbidden to eat crab—fresh cold crab with mayonnaise—or lobster—soft tender morsels of lobster dipped in melted butter. You don't even understand a simple thing like that, and yet you hope to discover why there are more Jews named Miller than Katz? Fat chance.

Anyway, here is a list of some of the most common crypto-Jewish names (as they're known in the Jewish Studies biz). Actually, it's pure guesswork on my part that these are the most common ones. They're just the first ones I thought of. You spend thirty, forty dollars on a big, beautiful, complete Jewish encyclopedia bound in leather and maybe there you'll find a scientific, scholarly discussion of the most common names. But here, for $2.75—feh!

So, anyway, if you meet a guy with one of the names on the list below, be very, very suspicious if he starts talking about how he rowed crew at Yale, or if he invites you to play a little squash down at his club. What's he trying to prove? Slip a word like **plotz** into your conversation and see if he hesitates a second before asking, "Huh? What did you say?" Or talk disparagingly about Albert Einstein: "Sure, he was bright, but it really makes me sick how he let his body get out of shape." There are many other tests, too numerous to go into here.

So here's the list (I've left off names that are technically Anglo-Saxon but *everyone* with that name is Jewish, like Singer and Glass and Gross):

Allen, Black, Brown, Brooks, Burns, Cane, Davis, Eastman, Ellis, Field(s), Garfield, Gladstone, Gordon, Grant, Green(e), Grey, Harris, Howe, Kane, King, Lewis, Lynn,

Lyons, May, Modigliani, Nichols, Miller, Mills, Morris, Morse, Moss, Nelson, Newman, Newton, Paul, Phillips, Rivers, Rose, Ross, Smith, Stone, Wallace and Warner.

There are also crypto-goyish names; the most common is probably Swartz (pronounced Schwartz). I hasten to assure you that Fred Swartz of the Christian Anti-Communist Crusade is not Jewish, nor are most people named Swartz.

Khan is another example—don't confuse it with Kahn. Actually, Genghis Khan took his last name from that of a man he greatly admired—Henry Kahn, his dentist. But being an illiterate Mongol horseman, he mispelled it.

D

dairy restaurant, dairy lunch
A Jewish restaurant that serves no meat, but more than makes up for it with a whole slew of exquisite delicacies you can't get in a deli—cheese blintzes, vegetarian chopped liver, rice pudding, etc.

B&H Dairy Lunch on Second Avenue in New York is the best dairy restaurant in the world (in terms of food) and the worst restaurant of any kind in the world (in terms of making it possible for you to digest that food). But it *is* entertaining. And oy—the kugel, the borsht...!

deli, delicatessen
For those of you who live in the Gobi Desert or on Mars and don't know what a delicatessen is, it's a store that sells all kinds of prepared dishes and meals. It usually doubles as a restaurant.

A kosher deli sells only flayshedika (qv) or pareve (qv) foods—that is, nothing containing milk. You have to go to a dairy restaurant (qv) for milk dishes.

Delicatessen means "delicate eating." I mention this because you wouldn't know it from eating in a lot of them.

der emes iz der bester ligun (dayr EH-mis iz dayr BES-ter LIG-un)
The truth is the best lie.

derma (DER-muh)
Kishka (qv).

der mensch is vos er iz, ober nisht vos er iz geven (dayr MENSH iz VAWS ayr IZ, AW-bayr NISHT VAWS ayr iz guh-VEN)

A man is what he is, not what he has been.

der zoyerer frukht halt zikh shtark oyfen boym; der zieser falt fun klensten vintel arop (dayr ZOY-ayr-er FRŎŎKHT HAHLT zikh SHTAHRK OY-fen BOYM; dayr ZEES-er FAHLT fawn KLEN-stun VINT-ul uh-RAWP)

The bitter fruit holds tight to the branch; the sweet falls off in the softest breeze.

I'd explain this one for you, but I haven't the slightest idea what it means. Or, rather, I have a dozen ideas about what it means. It sure is pretty though.

die liebe iz zies, nor zie iz gut mit broyt (dee LEE-buh iz ZEES, nawr zee iz GŎŎT mit BROYT)

Love is sweet, but it's good with bread. (You can't live on love alone.) You got it without the explanation, didn't you?

dill pickle (See **kosher dill**)

don't ask!

Standard answer to any question of the form: "How's your (business, health, whatever)?"

Ben and Hyman meet in the street. They exchange a few pleasantries and then Ben says, "Every time we talk it's this superficial chitchat. You never ask me anything about myself, how I'm feeling, how my business is doing, what's happening with my family. Don't you care about me, Hyman? Don't you care even enough to ask?"

Hyman is flabbergasted. What an outpouring of emotion! Consumed with guilt, he says, "Of course I care about you, Ben. How can you think I don't? Please, tell me, how's business? How's your lovely wife Shirley, your son Arnold, your daughter Elyse? How's your health? How've you been feeling?"

"Don't ask!"

don't be a stranger
Jewish equivalent of "y'all come n' see us when y' can."

doven (DUH-, DAW- or DAH-vun)
To pray, particularly in the traditional Jewish manner— rhythmically nodding and beating one's chest with a prayer book while chanting in a singsong.

draydel (see **dredl**)

draykup (DRAY-kup or -kawp)
1. Someone who confuses you, who makes your head spin.
2. Thus, a swindler; a con man.
3. Someone who bothers you, pesters you.
4. Someone who is confused, whose own head is spinning. (From the German for (literally) "spin-head.")

dreck
Crap, junk, worthless trash.
Ninety-nine percent of the output in any field is dreck.

dredl (DRAY-dul)
A dumb little square top that won't spin right that you're supposed to play with on Chanukah.

dybbuk (DIB-oŏk)
A spirit that possesses a living person.
Usually the soul of a dead person, it enters the body of someone who did it harm when it was alive. So be nice.

E

egg cream

A New York City soda fountain drink made with milk, flavored syrup (usually chocolate) and seltzer (carbonated water).

No eggs, no cream—though one theory has it that originally cream was used instead of milk and the name "egg cream" began as "ekht cream"—pure cream. This would explain how the word "egg" got in there, since everyone agrees that egg creams never had any eggs in them.

ekht

Pure; real.

-ele (see -ala)

emes (EHM-ess)

Truth.

Also used as an exclamation, in much the same way as *honest!, verdad!* or *c'est vrai!*

This is 100 percent pure Colombian—emes!

enema

With chicken soup and nakhes from your children, one of the three great Jewish cure-alls.

The house is packed as the hit Broadway show nears the end of the second act. Suddenly the star, a man in his fifties, clutches his chest and falls to the stage. The house lights go on and a doctor rushes up to help him. As the doctor begins administering CPR, as the audience sits in shocked silence, the voice of a middle-aged Jewish woman rings out from the balcony: "Give him an enema!"

This is ignored by everybody in an embarrassed silence. By now the doctor is injecting adrenalin directly into the actor's heart. An oxygen mask has been brought out from backstage. Again the yenta yells, "Give him an enema!"

The doctor winces and continues to work. About half the audience turns to give the woman a stare that would fuse steel. The oxygen mask is ready, but the doctor waves it away. Shaking his head sadly from side to side, he stands up and begins rebuttoning his cuffs. For a third time, the woman bellows, "Give him an *enema!*"

The doctor can't take any more. He turns toward the balcony and says in the coldest possible tone, "Madam, this man has just suffered a massive coronary. I can assure you that giving him *an enema,* as you suggest, would do him no earthly good at all."

From the balcony the voice comes back, "It couldn't hurt."

eppis (EH-pis)
1. Something. *Eat eppis, darling. You're all skin and bones.*
2. Really; quite. *Now is that eppis a noodle kugel, or what?*
3. Any kind of. *Who has eppis a suggestion?*
4. For some reason I can't put my finger on. *Eppis I don't feel like it.*

erev yontif, erev shabbes (AYR-uv YUN-tif, SHAH-buhs)
The afternoon before a holiday (yontif) or the sabbath (shabbes).

More or less equivalent to "the eve of," but since Jewish days begin at sunset (actually, when the stars come out),

Friday evening is not erev shabbes—it's shabbes itself. Erev shabbes is Friday *before* sunset.

The same is true of erev yontif, the afternoon before a holiday. What a wonderful time that is!—the smell of food cooking, the whole house being cleaned and aired out, everybody getting ready, waiting for the family to come over...

ess

Eat.

Well, what are you waiting for?

(Also see **fress.**)

ess, ess, mein kint! (ESS, ESS, mein kint)

Eat, eat, my child! (You're all skin and bones.)

This is sometimes rendered as S.S. Mein Kint, which conjures up visions of a ship with chubby-cheeked little boys and girls rolling around the decks. Lifeboats aren't needed because all the passengers float like corks.

F

far-

For words beginning **far-**, see **fer-** (except for **far** and **farfel**).

far dem emes shlogt men (fahr dem EH-mis SHLAWGT MEN)

For the truth, you get beat up.

farfel (FAHR-ful)

Noodle flakes about the size of grains of rice.

far dem emes shlogt men

far vos? (fahr VAWS)
Why?

faygala (FAY-guh-luh)
A male homosexual.
(Literally, "little bird.")

feh!
Phooey! An expression of disgust or disdain.

feinschmecker (FEIN-shmehk-ur)
A gourmet.
(Literally, "fine-taster," from the German.)

ferbissina (fer-BIS-in-uh)
Embittered, sour.

ferbissiner (fer-BIS-in-er)
Someone who is ferbissina.
(Also see **fertoutst**.)

ferbissiner

ferblunjit (fer-BLUN- or -BLAWN-jit)
Lost; mixed up.
(Also see **fertoutst**.)

ferchadit (fer-CHAH-dit)
Mixed up; confused.
(Also see **fertoutst**.)

fercockt, fercockta (fer-KAHKT, fer-KAHKT-uh)
More or less equivalent to "fucked up." (Literally, "shitted up.")
(Also see **fertoutst**.)

ferdrayt (fer-DRAYT)
Dizzy; confused.
William Kotzwinkle's *The Fan Man* is a brilliant portrait of a man who's ferdrayt.
(Also see **fertoutst**.)

fermisht (fer-MISHT)
Mixed-up.
(Also see **fertoutst**.)

ferpachkit (fer-PAHCH-kit)
Messed up.
(Also see **fertoutst**.)

fershimilt (fer-SHIM-ilt)
Moldy, gone bad.
(Also see **fertoutst**.)

fershlepta (fer-SHLEPT-uh)

Long, drawn-out.

Usually in the expression *a fershlepta krenk* (a long, drawn out illness), which is used to refer to anything—not just an illness—that drags on.

(Also see **fertoutst**.)

Here's a joke that's a little fershlepta, but well worth the time you spend with it. It's unquestionably the greatest salesman joke ever:

Irv is a buyer for a large department store. Al has been selling him a line of sporting goods for thirty years. One day Al comes in and tells Irv he's retiring.

"Mazel tov," says Irv. "What are your plans?

"Well, I've always been fascinated with Africa. Since Doris has passed away, there's really nothing to stop me from going there and seeing what it's like. I'm just going to poke around and see what I find."

Years go by and no one hears from Al. Finally the time comes for Irv to retire. For a long time, he's been an avid amateur entomologist. So he says to himself: you know there are a lot of interesting insects in Africa. It might be nice to go and check some of them out. Who knows, maybe while I'm there, I'll run into Al.

Irv has a wonderful time in Africa, discovering new bugs, but sees no sign of Al. Then one day, as he and his safari are traveling through a remote part of the bush, they see a scrawny man coming down the road toward them. He's dressed in rags; his hair is long and matted; flies are buzzing all around him. Suddenly, this bizarre creature shouts, "Irv!"

Who could this be? Irv wonders. Oh, no, that's impossible . . . But, sure enough, as the ragged man comes closer, Irv can see that beneath the face caked with dirt, this is indeed his old friend Al.

"Al," he says, "where have you been? No one's heard

from you in years. What are you doing out here in the middle of nowhere?"

"I've just gone native, I guess. The more time I spent here, the more I liked it. I live in that village over there. But what are *you* doing here?"

"Me? I'm an entomologist and..."

"Entomologist? What's that?"

"We study bugs."

"Bugs?" Al laughs. "What's there to study about bugs?"

"Bugs are very interesting!" Irv protests.. "Some bugs are very rare, *and* very valuable. For example," he says, picking a bug off of Al's chest, "if this one had red eyes instead of green, it would be worth about five hundred dollars."

"No kidding! That's incredible!" Al picks a bug from behind his ear and asks, "What about this one?"

"Ah, *that* one!" says Irv, warming to the subject. "If *that* one had four wings instead of two, it would be worth at least a grand."

And so for the next half hour, Al picks bugs off his body and Irv tells him what they're worth. But the sun is beginning to sink and Irv's safari has to move on in order to make camp before dark.

"Well, Irv," says Al, "it's been a real pleasure seeing you. Drop by and say hello when you come back this way."

"Al, it's been great to see you too. I'll let all the people back home know you're OK."

The two friends part and begin going their separate ways. After a few steps, Al stops, turns, and says, "Oh, and . . . Irv?"

"Yeah?"

"Thanks for looking at my line."

fershlugina, fershluginer
(fer-SHLŎOG-in-uh, fer-SHLŎOG-in-er)
Originally equivalent to "beat up." Now usually just means messed up, no good.
(Also see **fertoutst**.)

fershtay?, fershtayst? (fer-SHTAY?, -SHTAYST?)
Yiddish for *capeesh?* Do you understand? No, no, I'm not *asking* you if you understand. I'm telling you that fershtay? means "do you understand?" Capeesh?

39

fershtinkina, fershtunkina (fer-SHTINK-or-SHTŎONK-in-uh)
Lousy, stinking.
(Also see **fertoutst**.)

fershtinkiner, fershtunkiner (fer-SHTINK- or -SHTŎONK-in-er)
A stinker; a louse.

fershvitst (fer-SHVITST)
Sweated-up.

fertoutst (fer-TŎOTST)
Bewildered, mixed-up.
That ferbissiner! I ask him what he thinks of the situation and he says, "What do I think of this fershlugina, fershtinkina, fershlepta situation? I'll tell you what I think of it. I think it's fershimilt, ferpachkit and fercockt!" Then ten minutes later, he comes back and says he feels OK about it. I tell you, Irving, he's got me totally fermisht, ferdrayt, ferchadit, ferblunjit, fertummelt and fertoutst!

fertummelt (fer-TŎOM-ilt)
Befuddled; confused.
(Also see **fertoutst**.)

flanken (FLAHNK-un)
Meat from the flank of a steer, popular as a soup meat. Generally served with horseradish (khŕayn).

flayshedik, flayshedika, flayshik (FLAYSH-uh-dik, -dik-uh, FLAYSH-ik)
Containing meat or poultry.
It's not kosher to eat flayshedika foods with dairy foods.
(Opposite: **milchedik**. See **kosher** for details.)

the four questions (see **mah nishtana**)

fress
   To eat like an animal; that is, to eat quickly, noisily and in great quantity.
   (Compare with **ess**, to eat like a human being.)

fresser (FRESS-ur)
   A glutton; someone who makes a pig out of (usually him)self.

from that you make a living?
   The correct response to someone who tells you they're an artist, a musician, a writer or a blue-collar worker.
   An old Jewish man reads about Einstein's theory of relativity in the newspaper and asks his scientist grandson to explain it to him.
   "Well, zayda, it's sort of like this. Einstein says that if you're having your teeth drilled without Novocain, a minute seems like an hour. But if you're sitting with a beautiful woman on your lap, an hour seems like a minute."
   The old man considers this profound bit of thinking for a moment and says, "And from this he makes a living?"

frosk (frahsk)
   A slap, usually to the face, as in *frosk in pisk*, a smack in the kisser.
   Some people say **trosk** (trahsk).
   (Also see **potch**.)

funfer, fumfer (FUN- or FUM-fer)
   1. To talk through your nose.
   2. To fumble or stumble over your words.
   3. Someone who fumfers.
   4. Someone who's indecisive; a fence-sitter.
   5. Someone who's always making excuses.

G

Galitzianer (guh-LITZ-ee-AHN-er)

A Jew from Galicia, a province controlled at various times by both Poland and Austria.

In the prestige hierarchy of American Jews, as I learned it (it varies from group to group and person to person), the Portuguese Jews look down on the Spanish Jews who look down on the Austrian Jews who look down on the German Jews who look down on the Litvaks who look down on the Russian Jews who look down on the Ukrainian Jews who look down on the Polish Jews who look down on the Hungarian Jews who look down on the Roumanian Jews who look down on the Galitzianers who claim that they're Austrian.

ganze (GAHN-suh)

Total; whole.

ganze macher (GAHN-suh MAHKH-ur)

A big wheel; a VIP.

(Also see **macher**.)

gay

Go.

gay gezunt; gay gezunterhayt (GAY guh-ZŎONT, GAY guh-ZŎONT-er-hayt)

Go in health.

(Also see **zei gezunt**.)

gay in drerd arein (GAY in DRAYRD uh-REIN)

Go to hell. (Literally, "go into the ground.")

gay shlafen (GAY SHLAHF-un)

Go to sleep.

Now doesn't "gay shlafen" have a softer, more soothing sound than the harsh, staccato "go to sleep"? Listen to the difference:

Go to sleep, you little wretch!...Gay shlafen, darling.
Obvious, isn't it?

Clearly, the best thing you can do for your children is to start speaking Yiddish right now and never speak another word of English as long as you live. This will, of course, entail teaching Yiddish to all your friends, business associates, the people at the supermarket, and so on, but that's just the point. It has to start with committed individuals and then grow.

If your resolve should waver, just remind yourself what a happier, more joyous world it will be when everyone— African farmers, Filipino guerrillas, hunter-gatherers in Patagonia—speaks Yiddish. All over the world, the last words little children hear at night will be "gay shlafen, Maria-Teresa," "gay shlafen, Abdul," "gay shlafen, Wong...."

Why is it, when what needs to be done to bring world peace is so apparent, that there are still people who insist on following the old ways, ways that have been tried and have failed? For millennia children have been put to bed with "tais toi, morveux!", "callate, piojo!" and "shut uppa you face!" Isn't it time we tried a new approach?

Some minor adjustments will have to be made, of course: those signs written in what look like Yiddish letters won't be funny when everything is written in Yiddish. And we'll have to start driving on the left side of the road so we won't be reading the street signs backward. But is that too high a price to pay for world peace? I think not, my friend, I think not.

gay vays!

Go know! (Who could have known *that?!*)

Said when something so unexpected happens there was no way of predicting it.

gedempte flaysch (guh-DEMP-tuh FLAYSH)

Pot roast.

gefilte fish (guh-FIL-tuh FISH)

Patties made from ground fish (usually whitefish, pike and/or carp), eggs, onions, matza meal or matza crumbs (some people leave this out) and seasoning.

Gefilte fish is eaten hot or cold, usually with horseradish (khrayn). I like it with A-1 sauce (gottenyu!).

(Gefilte is German for "stuffed"—from the old practice of wrapping the skin of the fish around the patties before baking them.)

gehenna (guh-HEN-uh)

Hell.

(From the Hebrew *gehinom*, a valley south of Jerusalem where, in ancient times, children were sacrificed to the god Moloch.)

The ideas of heaven and hell play a very small part in the Jewish religion. But this wasn't the case with my aunt Sadie. She was so certain there's a life after death that when her husband was on his deathbed, she said: "Saul, please, after you're gone, try to communicate with me from the beyond."

And sure enough, about a week after the funeral, her phone rings, and it's Saul on the line! "Saul!" she says. "It's so good to hear from you! What's it like there?"

"It's not bad," Saul says. "I get up in the morning, make love, have a little something to eat, make love, have lunch, make love once or twice, take a short nap, make love again, eat dinner, make love three or four times, and go to sleep."

"So that's what heaven is like?" Sadie asks.

"What do you mean, heaven? I'm a bull in Wyoming."

gelt

Money.

Gemora (guh-MAW-ruh)

The newer of the two main sections of the Talmud (qv). Written in Aramaic between about 1700 and 1500 years ago, it consists of explanations of the Mishnah (qv), which itself consists of explanations of the Torah. The Gemora also contains parables, jokes, and the most rambling discourses conceivable.

genug (guh-NOOG)

Enough, as in *genug shoyn!*—enough already!

geshmak, geshmakta (guh-SHMAHK, -SHMAHK-tuh)

Mouth-wateringly delicious.

gesundheit (guh-ZOONT-heit)

Something you say after someone sneezes.

This is really a German expression, but I put it in because Jews use it too. What the hell, it only takes a couple of lines.

gevalt! (geh-VAHLT or -VAWLT)

A strong exclamation, more or less equivalent to "Oh my God!" most commonly heard in the expression *oy, gevalt!*

The first word we had for God I think was "gevalt." I mean—the lightning—we went already "gevalt!" (Mel Brooks).

gezunt (guh-ZOONT)

Health, as in *a gezunt af...* or *an* (uh guh-ZOONT ahf, ahn)—"a health on..."

45

For example, if a child says something nice about you, you might say, *a gezunt af dayn piskela* (dayn PISK-uh-luh)— a health on your little mouth. Other things that commonly get a gezunt put on them are *dayn shayna keppela* (dayn SHAY-nuh KEP-uh-luh)—your pretty little head, and *dayn pupik* (Dayn PŎOP-ik)—your bellybutton.

Health is a Jewish obsession, to the point where the signs in El Al planes read:

FASTEN YOUR SEAT BELT.
EXTINGUISH ALL SMOKING MATERIALS.
EAT FRUIT.

And it was on El Al that I heard the following announcement: "If your cabin pressure should drop, oxygen masks will appear below the overhead panels. To put them on, just slip this strap over your head. It's extremely unlikely you'll need to put the oxygen masks on; however, if they should become necessary, please, wear them in the best of health."

(Also see **a bi gezunt, gay gezunt, tsu gezunt** and **zei gezunt**.)

glitch

In computers, a false signal that causes the system to crash.

In printing, a blotch on a typeset letter, caused usually by dust on the negative.

Literally, a "slip" (in German).

glitzy (GLITS-ee)

Flashy in a tacky way, like a dress completely covered with sequins.

glot kosher (GLAHT KO-shur)

Strictly kosher. Shokhets (qv) are required to inspect the lungs of animals they slaughter. If they find tuberculosis nodules, the meat is trayf (not kosher). If they find the scars of healed tuberculosis nodules, the meat is kosher. If they find neither nodules nor scars, the lung is smooth (glot) and the meat is glot kosher.

Today the term is used to indicate not only this procedure but all of the most scrupulous kosher standards. Very orthodox Jews will only eat glot kosher meat.

God gives burdens; also shoulders

Jimmy Carter cited this Jewish saying in his concession speech at the end of the 1980 election. At least he said it was a Jewish saying; I can't find it anywhere. I'm sure he's telling the truth though; why would he lie about a thing like that?

golem, goylem (Go- or GOY-lum)

A robot, or a zombie in the sense of a corpse brought to life, like Frankenstein's monster. In fact, Mary Shelley may have gotten the idea for her book from a Jewish legend about Rabbi Loew of Prague who, in the sixteenth century, made a golem out of clay and brought it to life by placing a piece of paper in its mouth on which was written the secret name of God (sort of like a walking mezuzah).

Also, a clod or simpleton; anyone who acts like a lifeless, spiritless creature.

(From the Hebrew.)

gonif (GAHN-if)

1. A thief.
2. A chiseler or clever trickster.
3. Sometimes gonif just implies ingenuity, without any connotation of dishonesty. This is usually when referring to a child, or in the wonderful expression *America gonif!* which means "only in America could there be such cleverness!"

So you see, zayda, you just talk to this plastic statue and then drive over there to pick up your food.

   America gonif!

   Everybody's been a gonif at one time or another. There's
the wonderful story of two partners in the garment district
in New York. Neither one of them had taken a vacation in
twenty years. Finally Izzy's wife drags him away to Florida.
But he can't stop thinking about the business. So the first
day he's down there, he calls his partner Sam to see how
things are doing.

   "Izzy," says Sam, "the most terrible thing has happened.
Last night, right after you left, some burglars broke in and
stole the entire week's receipts!"

   "Sam," says Izzy calmly, "put it back."

gornisht (GAWR-nisht)
   Nothing.

gornisht helfen (see **'svet gornisht helfen**)

gornisht mit gornisht (GAWR-nisht mit GAWR-nisht)
   Worthless, useless.
   (Literally, "nothing with nothing.")

gott (gawt)
   God.
   "Why the people of Israel adhered to their God all the
more devotedly the worse they were treated by him is a
question we must leave open" (Sigmund Freud).

gottenyu! (GAHT- or GAWT-en-yoo)
   Dear God!
   Sort of a diminutive form of "Oh, my God!", not as
heavy as gevalt. *Gottenyu, what a haircut!*

gott iz an alter kuntsenmacher (GAWT iz ahn AHL-ter KŎŎNTS-en-MAHKH-er)

God is an old trickster.

gott vet helfen—vie helft nor gott biz gott vet helfen (GAWT vet HELF-un—vee HELFT nawr GAWT biz GAWT vet HELF-un)

God will provide—if only God would provide until God provides.

goy; plural: **goyim** or **goys;** adjective: **goyisha** or **goyish** (GOY-um, goyz, GOY-ish-uh, GOY-ish)

1. A non-Jew (non-Jews, not Jewish).

2. Someone resembling non-Jews as Jews have typically perceived them; therefore, someone who is stupid, insensitive or violent (although the word is usually used today in a light, joking way).

The distinction between Jewish and goyish can be quite subtle, however, as the following quote from Lenny Bruce illustrates:

> I'm Jewish. Count Basie's Jewish. Ray Charles is Jewish. Eddie Cantor's goyish. The B'nai Brith is goyish. The Hadassah is Jewish. Marine Corps—heavy goyish, dangerous.
>
> Kool-Aid is goyish. All Drake's Cakes are goyish. Pumpernickel is Jewish and, as you know, white bread is very goyish. Instant potatoes—goyish. Black cherry soda's very Jewish. Macaroons are *very* Jewish. Fruit salad is Jewish. Lime Jell-O is goyish. Lime soda is *very* goyish. Trailer parks are so goyish that Jews won't go near them.
>
> Balls are goyish. Titties are Jewish. Mouths are Jewish. All Italians are Jewish. Greeks are goyish. Eugene O'Neill—Jewish. Dylan Thomas—Jewish. Steve Allen is goyish, though. It's the hair. He combs his hair in the boys' room with that soap all the time.
>
> See how easy it is? Fidel Castro? Jewish, of course.

Henry Kissinger—goyish. Marlon Brando—Jewish. Ringo is Jewish. Paul is goyish. George is goyish. John, of course, was Jewish.

Talk is Jewish. Silence is goyish. Thin is goyish. Fat is Jewish. Blue is Jewish. Green is goyish. Atheism is Jewish. Converting to Christianity is, of course, goyish. But as R. Crumb points out, so is converting to Judaism. In fact, it's such a goyish thing, no Jew has ever done it.

Jewish   **goyish**

Computers are Jewish. Rifles are goyish. California is goyish. France is Jewish. The thirties were Jewish. The forties were goyish. The fifties were goyish. The sixties were Jewish. The seventies were goyish. The eighties are off to an intensely goyisha start.

Teddy Kennedy is Jewish. Ronald Reagan is goyish. Nancy Reagan is the most goyisha person who has ever lived. Marie Osmond is second. Tricia Nixon is third. David Eisenhower is like a broad caricature of a goy. Richard Nixon, however, is too much of an open maniac to be a goy.

OK, now you try it. One of the items in each pair listed

below is Jewish, and the other one is goyish. Can you tell which is which?

bowling alleys/constant guilt
Spam/chicken soup
crew cuts/big, dark, almond-shaped eyes
jumping out of planes/double-entry bookkeeping
respecting your scoutmaster/believing you're Jesus Christ

Goyim is the more common plural, and is always used when speaking generally: *What can you expect from goyim?*

Goys is used to refer to particular people. *A couple of goys.*

One of the oldest problems puzzled over in the Talmud is: "Why did God create goyim?" The generally accepted answer is: *"Somebody has to buy retail."*

goyim nakhes (GOY-im NAHKH-us)

The kind of things that gratify the stereotypical goy—a beautiful new motor home, bagging the limit duck hunting, a promotion to major, etc.

(Also see **nakhes**.)

goyisha essen (GOY-ish-uh ES-un)

The kind of food no Jew would eat (I know, don't tell me, I've seen it too—some Jews are more goyish than the goyim)—like scrapple, chitlins, chipped beef, head cheese, pig's feet, etc. It makes me sick just to list them.

goyisha kup (GOY-ish-uh KUP)

1. Someone who does something stupid, not shrewd, or like a goy in some subtler way. *You paid how much for that!—oy, what a goyisha kup!*

2. Less commonly, such a person's actual head.

There are lots of jokes about goyisha kups, like the one about the merchant who lost money on every sale figured but made it up on the volume. My favorite is the one about the liberal German judge who is pleading with Adolf Hitler not to harm the Jews. "If you can't find any other reason, then spare them simply because they're so smart," he says.

"Smart!" Hitler says. "Who says they're so smart?"

"I'll prove it to you," says the judge. "Come with me." He takes Hitler to a small shop run by a Jew named Weiss.

"Mr. Weiss," he says, "we're looking for a left-handed beer stein. Would you happen to have one?"

Without batting an eye, Weiss says, "Possibly. Let me look." He goes to the back of the store, picks up a beer stein, turns it so the handle is facing left, and comes back out.

"Lucky you," he says. "I've got one."

Back on the street, the judge turns to Hitler and says, "You see what I mean?"

Hitler says, "What did that have to do with being smart? He just happened to have one in stock."

goyisha mazel (GOY-ish-uh MAH-zul)
Non-Jewish luck.

The theory is that the Jews have the brains but the goys have the luck. There's even a saying: "the more goyish, the more lucky."

Why do things go well for a Jew who converts to Christianity, but badly for a goy who becomes a Jew? Because the former has a yiddisha kup and goyisha mazel, while the latter has a goyisha kup and yiddisha mazel.

gregor (GREG-ur)

Unlike the dredl (qv), which is a disappointment, the gregor is a holiday toy that's really wonderful. The holiday in this case is Purim. Now Purim could really be a drag, because you have to sit and listen to this long story (see **Purim** for the story). It's read from a scroll called the **Megillah**, whence comes the expression **the whole megillah** (qv). You can't truly appreciate what "the whole megillah" means until you've sat through the whole Megillah.

Anyway, in His great wisdom, God has given Jewish children the gregor to make this ordeal bearable. It's a— how can I describe it? Well, it's a noisemaker, sort of in the shape of a flag on a short pole, and when you twirl the flag around the pole, it makes this terrific grating noise.

A guy named Haman is the villain of the Megillah, and whenever his name is mentioned in the telling of the story, all the kids get to twirl their gregors around and make an incredible racket until the adult reading the story gets them quieted down and continues. Sometimes Haman's name comes up in one sentence after another.

The gregor is like the Great Equalizer—it makes it more of an even contest between the adult having to put up with the gregors and the kids having to put up with the story.

greps

To belch; a belch.

gribbenes (GRIB-un-is)

Crisp bits of chicken skin (usually with little pieces of

53

onion) left over from the rendering of chicken fat (schmaltz).

Gribbenes get added to any chopped liver worthy of the name, and can also be mixed in with mashed potatoes, put on white bread or (gasp) eaten by themselves. (This last option is only for the kind of person who eats peanut butter with a spoon.)

guilt

The Jewish mascot emotion.

As American as cherry pie; as Jewish as guilt.

Much has been written about the origins of Jewish guilt, but it seems pretty obvious to me—I mean, we killed him, didn't we? What's the sense of pretending? We're not fooling anybody.

As far as I know, Lenny Bruce was the first Jew to admit it publicly:

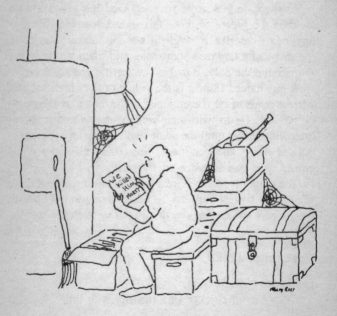

You and I know what a Jew is—One Who Killed Our Lord. I don't know if we got much press on this in Illinois—we did it about two thousand years ago—two thousand years of Polack kids whacking the shit out of us coming home from school. Why do you keep breaking our balls for this crime?

"Because you skirt the issue. You blame it on Roman soldiers."

All right. I'll clear the air once and for all, and confess. Yes, we did it—my family. I found a note in my basement that said:

"We killed him. (signed) Morty."

A lot of people say to me: "Why did you kill Christ?"

"I dunno . . . it was one of those parties, it got out of hand, you know."

We killed him because he didn't want to become a doctor, that's why.

H

If you don't find a word you're looking for under H, also check under **KH** or **CH**.

Hadassah (huh-DAH-suh)

An American women's Zionist organization, founded in 1912. It supports child welfare and medical services in Israel (like the Hadassah hospital in Jerusalem), and educational activities in the United States. It also provides "Hadassah ladies" with a wonderful opportunity for socializing.

Haggadah (huh-GAHD-uh)

What gets read (or read in part) at a seder (qv).

(Also see **Passover**.)

(From a Hebrew word meaning "the telling.")

haimish (see **haymish**)

hak (see **hok**)

half-done or **half-sour** (pickle)

This is the best way to eat a kosher dill—when it's still crunchy, light green, yet full of garlic flavor. The difference between this and the typical soggy, dark green cucumber corpse is like the difference between life and death.

You may find it difficult to find a good half-done kosher dill there in Seattle, so what you should do is take a cab

out to the airport, fly to New York, take the JFK Express
to Jay Street-Borough Hall, transfer to an uptown F, get off
at East Broadway, walk north on Essex (along the park),
make your first left onto Hester Street, walk about fifteen
steps, turn ninety degrees left, and stop. Say to the man,
"Let me have a nice half-done."

Worth the trouble, wasn't it?

halla (see **challah**)

halvah (HAHL-vah)
Look, this is crazy. Why am I *defining* halvah for you?
It's sold at every candy counter in the world. Oh, there
might be a 7/11 in Alabama or somewhere that doesn't have
it, but buying halvah isn't exactly like finding the Holy
Grail. So just go down to the corner, buy some, and eat it.
Now you know what halvah is. (And if I'd said: "a con-
fection made of ground sesame seeds and honey," you
wouldn't have known what it is—not really.)

Halvah is originally a Turkish delicacy, but it's hard to
imagine that Turks have eaten more of it than Jews. It's
like the Bible (only in reverse): the Jews invented it, but it
was the goyim who really ran with it.

Haman (HAY-min)
Famous bad guy. (See **Purim**.)

handler (HAHND-ler)
A sharp business person; a trader; a dealer.

Hanukah (see **Chanukah**)

Hassid, Hassidim (see **Chassid**)

haymish, haymisha (HAY-mish, HAY-mish-uh)
Homey, "down-home," informal, comfortable.

57

hays
> Hot—in its literal, figurative and sexual senses.

herring
> This delightful fish comes in many varieties: *matjes*, *schmaltz*, *marinirta*, etc. It can be eaten in a salad, all by itself, or *gehakta* (chopped up) and mixed with onion, bread, apple and vinegar. Herring also comes in wine sauce and— my hands are trembling—in cream sauce.
>
> To know what herring in cream sauce is really like, you have to go to Barney Greengrass' at 87th and Amsterdam in New York (although actually the kind you get in bottles at the supermarket isn't too bad; it's closer to the real thing than most store-bought Jewish foods).

the high holidays or high holy days
> Rosh Hashonah and Yom Kippur (qv).
> (Also see **shofer** and **kol nidre**.)

hok (hahk)
> To bother, pester, nag. (See **hok a chainik**.)

hok a chainik (or **hok mir a chainik** (HAHK (meer) uh CHEI-nik)
> 1. To talk someone's ear off.
> 2. To nag or pester.
> Literally, to hok a chainik means to "bang on a teakettle." Harold Eiser tells me that the expression comes from a common custom of the shtetl: when a woman had had all she could take of her family problems, she would walk out into the middle of the street and bang on her teakettle. Hearing this, the neighboring housewives would come out and listen while she told them her troubles. When she got it all off her chest, everybody would go home again.
> Isn't that wonderful?—instant group therapy, on demand. And you thought Fritz Perls invented it.

hok a chainik

hok mir nisht a chainik (HAHK meer NISHT uh CHEI-nik)

>Stop yakking at me. (I can't hear myself think.)
>Literally, stop banging on a teakettle.
>This expression is also heard as **hok mir nisht kayn chainik** (HAHK meer NISHT kayn CHEI-nik) and **hok nisht kayn chainik** (HAHK NISHT kayn CHEI-nik).

homentashen (HOM-in-TAHSH-in)

>Triangular cookies filled with fruit (usually prunes) or poppyseeds. Served on Purim or—by the truly enlightened—all year round. (The name means "Haman's pockets," after the Purim villain, although I don't know what his pockets have to do with anything.)

hoo-ha (hoo-hah)

>An exclamation, more or less equivalent to "oh, boy!"

Hoo-ha has become a noun in English, meaning a big tsimis.

houpie (see **khoupa**)

I

in drayrd arein (in DRAYRD uh-REIN)

Go to hell. (Literally, "into the ground." Short for **gay in drayrd arein**.)

is it good for the Jews?

After several thousand years of being knocked from pillar to post, it's not surprising that Jews tend to look at current events from this perspective. So does every other group, and most have less of a historical excuse for it.

Even so, it can be carried to extremes, as in Victor Fischer's *Windsurfing: Is It Good for the Jews?* or David Weidenfield's classic monograph, *Worldwide Nuclear War— Is It Good for the Jews?*

Is it good for the Jews?

J

JAP (acronym for **Jewish-American princess**)

Jewish princess, Jewish-American princess, Jewish prince

A "Jewish princess" is the product of a poorly understood process whereby a Jewish mother clones her personality and places it in the body of her daughter. Symptoms vary widely but always include manipulative self-centeredness and a compulsive need to redecorate.

Victims tend to be almost exclusively upper-middle class Americans. Other high-risk factors include marriage to a doctor or other professional, owning a Mercedes, and membership in a tennis club. It's not yet clearly understood whether these are causes or effects of the disease.

A similar disorder—known as JMDS (Jewish Mother's Darling Syndrome)—affects men. There is no known cure for either ailment.

Here's a joke about a Jewish prince:

A huge limousine rolls up to a luxury hotel. The chauffeur opens the left door and a middle-aged Jewish matron gets out. Then he rushes around to the right side, opens the door, reaches in, and emerges with a chubby Jewish boy, about twelve years old, in his arms. The boy is wearing an expensive suit, complete with a little cap and pearl gray gloves. He has a complaisant smirk on his face.

A yenta is watching all this from the sidewalk and says, "Oh, the poor boy! He can't walk!"

"Of course he can walk!" the boy's mother snaps at her. "Let's just hope he never has to."

jokes (Jewish)

Rather than try to attach every joke to a definition whether it fits or not, I've decided to be straightforward about it and put the extras here:

A man goes to a tailor to try on a new custom-made suit. The first thing he notices is that the arms are too long.

"No problem," says the tailor. "Just bend them at the elbow and hold them in front of you. See, now it's fine."

"But the collar is up around my ears!"

"It's nothing. Just hunch your back up a little...no, a little more...that's it."

"But I'm stepping on my cuffs!" the man cries in desperation.

"Nu, bend your knees a little to take up the slack. There you go. Look in the mirror—the suit fits perfectly."

So, twisted like a pretzel, the man lurches out onto the street. Reba and Florence see him go by.

"Oh, look," says Reba, "that poor man!"

"Yes," says Florence, "but what a beautiful suit."

Murray and Esther, a middle-aged Jewish couple, are tour-ing Chile. Murray just got a new camera and is constantly snapping pictures. One day, without knowing it, he pho-tographs a top-secret military installation. In an instant armed troops surround Murray and Esther and hustle them off to prison.

They can't prove who they are because they've left their passports in their hotel room. For three weeks they're tor-tured day and night to get them to name their contacts in the liberation movement. Finally they're hauled in front of a military court, charged with espionage, and sentenced to death.

The next morning they're lined up in front of the wall where they'll be shot. The sergeant in charge of the firing squad asks them if they have any last requests. Esther wants to know if she can call her daughter in Chicago. The sergeant says he's sorry, that's not possible, and turns to Murray.

"This is crazy!" Murray shouts. "We're not spies!" And he spits in the sergeant's face.

"Murray!" Esther cries. "Please! Don't make trouble."

Many Jewish jokes have a bittersweet quality, but none so bittersweet as this one:

It's March 1940, at a Jewish refugee center in Paris. The woman in charge asks the first refugee:

"Where would you like to go?"

"London," he answers.

"How about you?" she asks the second.

"Sweden."

"And you?" she asks the third.

"New Zealand."

"New Zealand! Why so far?"

The refugee answers: "Far from what?"

Judesmo (see **Ladino**)

K

kaddish (KAH-dish)

One of several prayers praising God, most commonly the prayer for the dead. (Don't confuse kaddish with **kiddush,** a blessing said over the wine.)

Although the kaddish is used as a mourner's prayer, it makes no mention of death. The idea is that it's especially important to express one's faith in God at a time of deep loss.

Traditionally Jews are required to say kaddish every day for eleven months after the death of a parent or a child, and on every anniversary (**yortsite**) thereafter (and for a month after the death of a sibling or a spouse).

The first words of the kaddish are *yisgadal v'yiskadash*. Sometimes these are used humorously. For example, if you and a friend are watching a football game, and the team he's betting on has a one-point lead but fumbles on their own two-yard line with forty seconds left on the clock and the other team recovers, you might taunt him by chanting: "yisgadal v'yiskadash..."

The kaddish is a very beautiful prayer; the sound of the Aramaic words and the rhythm are deeply moving. Unlike the kol nidre, it's chanted rather than sung, but it's also worth listening to.

kadokhes (kuh-DO-khus)

Convulsions, as in *ikh vel im geben a kadokhes* (ikh vel

eem GAY-bun ah kuh-DO-khus)—I'll give him convulsions
(that's all he'll get from me—not a thing besides).

ka ka (kah kah)
Child's word for "shit."
Comes from the same German root that gives us **cocker,
cocked up, fercockt,** etc.

kasha (KAHSH-uh)
Kasha is always defined as "buckwheat groats." There's
only one problem with this definition: what the fuck are
"buckwheat groats"? *I* know what they are—they're kasha.
But that doesn't help you much.
It's like a sign I once saw in an elevator that read:

> TO ACTUATE ELEVATOR MECHANISM—
> 1. SELECT FLOOR DESIRED
> 2. DEPRESS BUTTON CORRESPONDING TO FLOOR DESIRED

Imagine the sort of person who can understand that, but
doesn't know how to push the buttons in an elevator. This
is the same person who knows what "buckwheat groats"
are. Now all we have to do is find him.

kasha varnishkas (KAHSH-uh VAHR-nish-kuz)
Kasha with noodles, onions, schmaltz or vegetable short-
ening, salt and pepper.

kashrus, kashruth (KAHSH-roos or -root)
Kosher-ness; keeping kosher (qv).

kayn
No, none.

KH
If you don't find the word you're looking for under KH,
also check under **H** and **CH**.

khad gadyaw (khahd-gahd-yaw)

The title and chorus of an extremely stupid song about a goat. It gets sung on Passover by little children who don't know any better.

khallah (see **challah**)

khaloshes (khah-LO-shus)

Awful; disgusting.

kharosis (khah-RO-sis)

One of the ritual foods eaten at the Passover seder. It's made of chopped apples and nuts, mixed together with sugar and wine. It's great.

khayder (see **cheder**)

khazen (see **cantor**)

khazer (see **chazer**)

khazerei (see **chazerei**)

kholeria (see **choleria**)

khometz, adjective: **khometzdik** (KHAW-mets, KHAW-mets-dik)

Isn't it strange that all those words related to Passover are coming one after the other? First **khad gadyaw,** then **kharosis,** now **khometz.** I wonder if it's a full moon? Let's see, Passover is an Aries...

Hmmm? Oh, yes, khometz. Well, on Passover you're not allowed to eat any kind of leavened bread—nothing, not even a Twinkie. It's strictly matza, Ak-Maks or those Scandinavian crackers that taste like cardboard. Leavened bread (along with all other forbidden stuff) is called khometz. Stuff that's OK is **pesadika**.

You have to clean out your house before Passover, sweeping up bread crumbs. God is very fussy about this; the house must be 100 percent free of khometz.

Right before Passover (aka Pesach), everything you buy in stores in New York starts being labeled "pesadika"— kosher for Pesach. Things you can't imagine *not* being kosher for Pesach—Brillo, celery, tampons—are labeled "kosher for Pesach." So if you're worried about something khometzdik accidentally being in your house during Pesach, all you have to do (in New York, at least) is throw everything out and buy new ones at the store the week before. This takes an enormous worry off your mind.

khoumish (KHOŎM-ish)

The Five Books of Moses (Genesis, Exodus, Leviticus, Numbers, and Deuteronomy).

(From the Hebrew word for "five.")

khoupie, khoupa (KHOŎ-pee, -puh)

The wedding canopy (not to be confused with the wedding canapés, which come later).

At Orthodox, Conservative and some Reform weddings, the bride and groom stand under a canopy supported by four poles. This symbolizes a room in the groom's house where, in ancient times, the bride and groom consummated their marriage.

Another custom is for the groom to break a glass under his foot. What do you suppose that stands for?

(Also see **no khoupie, no shtupie**.)

khoutspah (see **chutzpah**)

khrayn

Grated horseradish (often mixed with vinegar and/or beet juice).

kibbutz, plural: **kibbutzim** (ki-BOŌTS, ki-boŏt-SEEM)

A kind of cooperative farm found in Israel. (Don't confuse kibbutz with **kibitz,** to give unwanted advice.)

Kibbutzim vary in terms of how communal they are, but the most radical ones are probably more genuinely socialistic than any other institution in the world (including anything that exists in Communist countries).

For example, nowhere has communal child rearing been carried out in such a thoroughgoing manner, with children living with groups of their peers and under the supervision of "multiple mothers" from an extremely early age. The effects of this are almost entirely positive.

Most books on this subject are pretty terrible. A. I. Rabin's *Growing Up in the Kibbutz* is the best I've read. It has some defects, but compensates by being reasonably well organized and well written.

kibitz, kibitzer (KI-buts, KI-buts-ur)

A spectator who gives unwanted advice is a kibitzer. Typically, the activity kibitzed is chess or a card game, but it can be anything. (Don't confuse this with **kibbutz,** a kind of cooperative farm in Israel.)

To "kibitz around" means to joke with friends, or to socialize in a relaxed, purposeless way:

"What are you guys doing?"

"Nothing. Just kibitzing around." (This is an exact— although more polite—equivalent of *"Nothing. Just screwing around."*)

kichel, plural: **kichlach** (KIKH-il, KIKH-lahkh)

A little puffed-up cookie, made with a lot of egg and usually coated with sugar.

kiddush (KID-ish)

A prayer said over the wine at the beginning of the

sabbath and holidays. (Don't confuse kiddush with **kaddish,** a prayer for the dead.)

kina hora (KIN-uh HAW-ruh)
Also **kayn ayn hora** (KAYN ayn HAW-ruh).
Literally, no evil eye. It's used whenever the evil eye threatens, which is basically whenever you're saying things are good. *My little Marvin graduates dental school next month, kina hora.*

The idea is that if you show your happiness or pride too openly, someone will overhear you, become envious, and put the evil eye on you. I don't know exactly how you go about putting the evil eye on someone, but I think it's something like sticking pins in a voodoo doll, only without the pins or the doll.

Despite its spooky origins, kina hora is used exactly the way the English expression "knock on wood" is. "Knock on wood" probably goes back to some Druidic superstition too: *The spirit of the oak tree is pleased with us, knock on wood.*

kint; plural: **kinder;** affectionate plural: **kinderlach** (kint, KIN-der, KIN-der-lahkh)
Child, children.
I'm not a big fan of the theory that Yiddish has special nuances that can't be translated into English, although of course Yiddish words (like those of any language) have a flavor all their own, and lose something in translation.

But I must say that I didn't know how I can even begin to communicate to you the love and tenderness embodied in the word kinderlach. Any culture has its strong points (as well as its weak ones), and I guess love for children is a strong point of Jewish culture. (Another obvious one is love of knowledge.)

That's all you get. If you want a better feeling for the word kinderlach, you'll just have to listen to Jews use it.

kishka (KISH-kuh)

Meat, flour and seasonings stuffed into the intestines of a steer and baked. (It tastes better than it sounds.)

(From the Russian for intestines.)

kishkas (KISH-kuz)

Guts, as in the classic piece of ringside advice: *hit him in the kishkas!*

kish mir in tokhis (KISH meer in TAW-khis)

Kiss my ass.

klop (klahp)

A blow, as in a *klop in kup,* a smack in the head. A klop can be quite hard. *I'll give you such a klop your ears will ring!*

(Also see **potch**.)

klutz (kluhts)

A klutz.

knadl, plural: **knadlach** (KNAYD-ul, KNAYD-lakh)

A matza ball (qv).

knish (knish, *not* kuh-nish)

Knishes vary so much in quality that it's hard even to figure out a definition that will cover the range—from the greasy New York subway killer knish (one bite causes stomach cancer) to Yonah Schimmel's exquisite creations. A knish *should* be a light, flaky pastry filled with kasha, mashed potatoes, chopped liver, cheese or—my hands are trembling—cheese with fruit.

A cherry cheese from Yonah Schimmel's (on Houston Street in New York) is right up there with sex, the Caribbean and foot massage. It's way beyond mere food.

Knish is also slang for "vulva." Which reminds me of a joke:

Mr. Shapiro goes to Dr. Rappoport for his yearly checkup.

"I have great news, Doctor," he says. "I'm getting married."

"Really?" says the doctor. "Mazel tov. Anyone I know?"

"Certainly it's someone you know. It's one of your patients. Bernie Cohen's widow, Bertha."

Bertha Cohen! thinks the doctor. I wonder if it's ethical ...? Well, it would be more unethical not to tell him ...

"Seymour, I think it's only fair to mention this to you. Bertha Cohen has acute angina."

"You're telling me!"

koch leffel (KAWKH lef-ful)

A busybody, a nosy gossip, someone who's always stirring up trouble. (Literally, a "cooking spoon" that you stir things with.)

kol nidre (kawl NID-ruh, KOHL NID-ray)

The first prayer of the Yom Kippur service.

It's sung to a melody on which Max Bruch and Arnold Schoenberg have based works. Snatches of the melody are also found in Beethoven's C Sharp Minor Quartet, Opus 131, and his Trio, Opus 9, Number 3.

The kol nidre has been the subject of a lot of debate, which isn't surprising, since it says: "All vows, obligations, oaths ... which we swear ... from this Yom Kippur to the next ... shall not bind us. May they be deemed null and void." Originally the wording referred to the year just finished, rather than the year to come. But, either way, does this mean that Jews don't have to worry too much about the promises they make, because their most sacred prayer absolves them from their obligations once a year?

Well, obviously not. Jews had enough trouble surviving stories about how they murdered Christian children and used their blood to make matza for Passover (which is ridiculous! only special matzas—marked XXX on the box—are made in this way); if we actually broke our promises every year, we never would have survived the pogroms.

If anything, Jews tend to regard obligations *more* solemnly than most people. And the kol nidre was opposed for just that reason by rabbis from as early as the ninth century. So what's it doing ushering in the most sacred holiday of the year?

Who knows? I don't understand it. The best explanation I've heard is that Jews have often been forced to convert to other religions, or to swear oaths under duress and in degrading circumstances: standing on a pigskin, in a bucket of water, wearing a crown of thorns, and so forth. The kol nidre forgave them for all these false vows.

The current interpretation is that the kol nidre absolves you from vows that don't involve other people (like New Year's resolutions) but not from obligations to others. If religion were rational, the kol nidre would be changed to reflect this interpretation. But it isn't, and no one wants to change a beautiful prayer that's thousands of years old.

(Kol nidre is Hebrew for "all vows.")

kop (see **kup**)

kosher (KO-sher—boy, if you don't know how to pronounce kosher, you *really* need this book)
1. OK, not forbidden.
2. Cooked in the Jewish manner ("kosher-style") as in "kosher dill."
3. The original meaning is "not forbidden to eat."

The rules governing what's kosher and what's not are very complex, and are ignored in part or in full by most Jews. But I can see you're curious, so here's a summary of them:

   1. You can't eat milk and meat at the same meal. Orthodox

Jews wait six hours after having eaten meat before they eat any dairy food, and a shorter time (which varies) before eating meat after dairy.

The basis for this is the Biblical commandment: "thou shalt not seethe [i.e. boil] a kid in its mother's milk." If this seems a somewhat tenuous line of reasoning to you, you're not alone. There was extensive Talmudic debate as to what those words mean; "don't add insult to injury" is one possible interpretation that has nothing to do with diet. But somehow the Talmudists came up with the milk/meat dichotomy.

I myself am a strict constructionist: I see nothing wrong with eating a chesseburger, but I will never, under any circumstances, eat baby goat that has been boiled in milk from its own mother. (Milk from *another* nanny goat— sure, no problem. This makes the delicious dish *chevreau au lait*.)

Anyway, kosher households have two complete sets of dishes, silverware and cooking utensils—one for dairy foods (**milchedika**) and one for meat (**flayshedika**). It's very bad to use the wrong kind of utensil.

Certain things—like vegetables, fruit and fish—are **par-eve** and can be eaten with either milk or meat.

2. You can't eat the meat of any four-legged animal unless it both chews its cud and has a cloven hoof. So pigs are out, since they don't chew their cuds (or anybody else's, for that matter). Horses are out, since their hooves are all in one piece.

3. Anything from the sea must have scales and fins, thus eliminating all shellfish (beginning to sound a little nuts, isn't it?).

4. Animals must be slaughtered according to certain ritual procedures by a **shokhet** (qv).

5. Birds of prey are out—no more owl stew.

6. Animals that crawl, like lizards or snakes, are **trayf** (not kosher).

7. That's pretty much it, except for some miscellaneous weird stuff: worms and weasels are forbidden, and so is flesh torn from a living animal (sorry about that) and—read it and weep—snails.

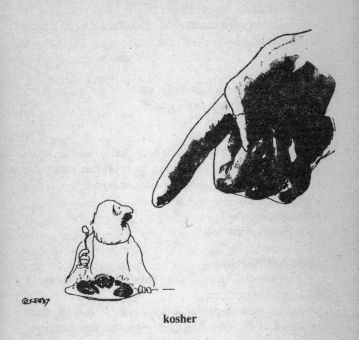

kosher

kosher dill

This is to a pickle what Beethoven's Ninth is to a symphony. I eat those "Polish-style pickles" and I think, "What is this, are they kidding? Talk about *goyisha essen!*"

Now I try to be fair about this kind of thing. When I was in France, I ate brains, lungs, anything. I love *sashimi*, *escargots*, guava chunks with *queso blanco*, *galactoboureko*, veal *piccata*, *pelmeny*, *gulab juman*—I'm not a parochial eater. And I think most Jewish food is dreck. But when it comes to pickles, there's nothing even close to a kosher dill.

Polish-style pickles—ha!

krank; krankheit (krahnk, KRAHNK-heit)
Sick; sickness.
Jews always get a chuckle out of Walter Cronkite's name for this reason.

krekhtz (krekhts)
A cross between a sigh and a groan.
Also, to make such a noise.
How are you doing?
Ehhhhhh.
A krekhtz can be a word or a phrase as well as just a sound. For example, after eating an enormous meal, you might krekhtz: *Oy, what have I done to myself?*

krenk (kraynk)
An illness, a disease.

kreplach (KREP-lahkh)
Jewish ravioli. That is, dumplings filled with cheese or meat, then boiled or fried.
Kreplach were considered a delicacy by Jews of the shtetl (compared to the even less interesting fare that composed the rest of their diet). Isaac Bashevis Singer quotes a proverb: "In time, one gets tired even of kreplach." In my experience, it doesn't take very long.
There's a wonderful joke about a kid who has a morbid fear of kreplach. His mother consults a psychiatrist, who suggests that she show him every step in the making of them, so he can see that his fear has no basis.
So she goes home, sits her son down at the kitchen table, and begins to make kreplach.

"Moishela, look, I'm chopping up the meat to make the filling. Nothing to be afraid of here, is there?"

"No, mama."

"Good. Now I'm going to roll out the dough, and cut it into the right shapes. Nothing to be afraid of here, is there?"

"No, mama."

"Fine. Now I'm spooning the filling into the pieces of dough. Nothing to be afraid of here, is there?"

"No, mama."

"*Very* good. Now we just fold the edges of the dough up over the filling, like this..."

"Yaaaaah!! Kreplach!!!!!"

Mary Roo

kugel (KOO- or KŎŎ- or KI-gul)

A pudding, usually of noodles or potatoes.

kuni lemel (KOO-nee LEM-ul)

A not-very-bright country bumpkin. (After Rakhoun

"Coony" Lemmel, well-known sportscaster of nineteenth-century Vilna.)

(Also see **shlemiel**.)

kup (kuhp, kawp)

Head.

kurva (KUR- or KOOR-vuh)

Whore.

kvell (kvel, *not* kuh-VEL)

To take extreme pride or pleasure in the accomplishments of others, typically one's children.

Kvelling can be competitive, as when two Jewish mothers talk about their respective sons:

First yenta: "My son? Ah, what an angel! You'd think that as head of cardiology at the medical center, he wouldn't have time for his poor old mother. But, no! He calls me every other day, and at least once a week he has dinner with me. Last year on my birthday he gave me a diamond ring worth six thousand dollars."

Second yenta: "Well, you certainly have a devoted son! In fact, I can't think of another to compare with him, except of course my little Bruce-ala. Not only does he call me *every* day, not only does he come over for dinner at least *twice* a week, but every morning he spends an hour talking to the most prominent psychiatrist in New York. One hundred dollars an hour he pays this man, and do you know what he talks about? *Me!*"

I think that if I go about it smoothly enough, I may be able to sneak in another shrink joke without your noticing that it has nothing at all to do with "kvell":

Attractive woman patient: "Doctor! Kiss me!"

Psychiatrist: "Kiss you?! Strictly speaking, I shouldn't

even be on the couch with you."

(From a German word meaning "to gush," "to swell.")

kvetch (kvech, *not* kuh-VECH)

A whining complainer.

Also, to whine and complain.

Franz Kafka is a good example of a kvetch. Here's a joke about another one:

Herschel and Chaim grew up together on the Lower East Side. Chaim was always a spiritual sort and when he was a young man, he left on a trip around the world to find the religious path that was right for him. He ended up in a Trappist monastery and eventually became its abbot.

Meanwhile, Herschel had been having a hard time of it. One business after another had failed; his first wife had died quite young; and his second wife had just left him about the time that Chaim came back to New York for a visit.

"Chaim," Herschel said, "my life is mess. Everything is like ashes in my mouth. You seem to be at peace with yourself. Tell me, what should I do?"

"Well, Herschel, I only know what's worked for me. You could become a novitiate in my order, but it won't be easy. We take a vow of silence. You'd only be allowed to speak two words every five years."

Herschel thinks it over, decides he has nothing to lose, and goes to live at the monastery where Chaim is abbot. Five years later, he goes to his first interview with Chaim. The two words he picks to speak are "no sex."

Another five long years go by, and he comes to see Chaim again. This time his two words are "bad food."

Five more years of backbreaking work and spartan living pass, and at the end of them, the two words Herschel picks are "hard bed."

After his twentieth year at the monastery, Herschel, now a white-haired old man, figures he's had enough. He goes to see Chaim and says, "I can't take it anymore. I'm going to leave."

"Well, Herschel, I'm sorry to see you go," Chaim says, "but I must say I'm not surprised. All you've done since you got here has been kvetch, kvetch, kvetch."

L

Ladino (luh-DEE-no)

The Sephardic equivalent to Yiddish. A mixture of Spanish and Hebrew (and some Arabic, Greek and Turkish) elements spoken by Mediterranean Jews and their descendants (although many in the United States switched over to Yiddish so they could communicate with their Ashkenazic neighbors).

(Also see **Sephardim**.)

lag tefillin (LAGH tuh-FIL-un)

To put on tefillin (qv).

landsman; plural: **landsleit** (LAHNTS-mun, -leit)

Someone who comes from the same town or village in Europe as you do (or whose family comes from the same town as your family does).

latka (LAHT-kuh)

A pancake, usually one made from grated potatoes fried in oil. Potato latkas are a traditional dish of Chanukah, but are commonly served all year round. They're really good with applesauce and/or sour cream.

le chaim (luh KHEIM)

A toast.

(It means "to life" in Hebrew.)

Litvak (LIT-vahk)

A Jew from Lithuania or the surrounding area. Litvaks have a reputation for being clever but unfeeling.

(Also see **Galitzianer**.)

lokh in kup (LAWKH in KUP or KAWP)

A hole in the head.

Heard almost exclusively in the expression: *This I need like a lokh in kup!*

loshen (LAW- or LUH-shun)

Language.

(Also see **mama loshen**.)

lox (lahks)

Smoked salmon.

(Also see **novy**.)

lozem gayn (LAW-zum GAYN)

Let him go. Forget it.

l'shona tova tikosavu (luh-SHO-nuh TOH-vuh tik-O SAY-voo)

Usually shortened to **l'shona tova**.

A Rosh Hashonah greeting that means "may you be inscribed for a good year (in the Book of Life)"—the idea being that each year God figures out who deserves to live out the year and writes down all their names.

I like the longer version better, because it sounds sort of exotic and Polynesian, rather than Jewish, to my ear (I'm not saying there's anything wrong with sounding Jewish, you understand, but Polynesian makes for a nice change of pace), and also because it reminds me of Rikki-Tikki-Tavi (who, of course, being a mongoose, wasn't Jewish either. Actually, all mongooses are Seventh Day Adventists, a fact you may not have known. If you think I'm making this up, ask yourself if you've ever seen a mongoose:

1. smoke a cigarette?
2. drink coffee?
3. drive a fast car with the top down and a loose-looking woman on his arm?)

But for me the interesting thing about this whole Book of Life idea is why God has to write the names down. I mean, it's such a *Jewish* concept: here's God—all-powerful, all-knowing—and he can't remember who's supposed to live and who's supposed to die. He has to write it down in his Week-at-a-Glance. "Monday—kill Lee Chung Wa, Rosaria Machado, M'bele Tuwumba...Don't forget the thunderstorms over Iowa. Pick up brown slacks from cleaners."

You can bet the goyisha God doesn't have to *write down* like some candy-ass who he's going to kill. Hell, no. He just rides in around sunset after a long day of mending fences and rescuing lost dogies, swings down off of his horse, hitches his sunburned lean body up onto the top rail of the fence, rolls himself a cigarette, takes a long drag on it, pushes back the brim of his hat with his thumb, and says softly to himself in a deep, husky voice: "Well, let's see now. Guess I have to kill a couple hundred thousand of them. OK, how about you . . . you . . . that colored fellow over there, you, and you . . . yes, ma'am, I'm sorry . . . you, you . . ."

The Reagan god—he's so . . . sexy.

luftmensh (LŎOFT-mensh)

A dreamer; someone with no visible means of support; a jack-of-all-trades who makes a living at none.

(Literally, an "air person," someone whose head is in the clouds.) Noel Airman, in Herman Wouk's *Marjorie Morningstar*, is a luftmensch, as his name indicates.

lukshen; lukshen kugel (LUK-shin KOO-gul)

Noodle; noodle pudding.

lump (lŏomp)

A bum, a scoundrel.

M

macher (MAHKH-ur)

A big shot, a wheeler and dealer.

A real big shot is called a **ganze macher**.

mach shnel (mahkh SHNEL)

Hurry up. Make it fast.

mah nishtana hulaila huzeh mikawl hulaylos (mah nish-TAH-nuh huh-lei-luh huh-ZEH mi-KAWL huh-LAY-los, but I really need musical notation, since it's chanted and I can only hint at how it sounds with just upper- and lowercase letters to work with)

"Why is this night different from all other nights?" The first of the four questions asked on Passover, which the Haggadah answers.

Actually, there are four other questions (so it's really the five questions):

Why do we eat matza? (To remind us of the flight from Egypt and the unleavened bread the Hebrews ate during the forty years they spent in the wilderness.)

Why do we use bitter herbs? (To remind us of the bitterness of slavery.)

Why do we dip the bitter herbs in salt water? (To remind us of the tears the Hebrews shed while they were slaves in Egypt.)

Why do we lie down when we eat? (Well, we don't. Usually when this question is asked, everybody sort of slouches back in their chairs. But the reason we're *supposed* to eat lying down is that the seder—with its many different foods—is actually an imitation of a Greek feast, and the Greeks ate lying down.)

makhaiya (muh-KHEI-yuh)
A blessing (in the sense of a real joy).
Sinking into a hot bath after a long day, you might say: *Ah, what a makhaiya!*
(Makhaiya comes from the Hebrew *khai*—"life," as in **le chaim**.)

makher (see **macher**)

makhetunim (mah-khuh-TOON-im)
In-laws, but makhetunim usually means not just a few in-laws, but that whole side of the family. "In-laws" doesn't convey the feeling of an enemy army, or a horde, the way makhetunim does.

mamaleega (MAH-muh-LEE-guh)
Roumanian cornmeal mush.

mama loshen (MAH-muh LAW-shun)
Yiddish. Usually translated as "the mother tongue," it more probably means mother's tongue—the language mother uses—as opposed to Hebrew, the language father uses in shul and in his studies.

mamzer (see **momzer**)

mandelbrot (MAHN-dul-brawt)
Almond cake.

Marrano (muh-RAH-no)
A Spanish Jew forced to convert to Catholicism. Many Marranos practiced Judaism in secret.

Leo Rosten lists some of the methods used to convince Spanish Jews to convert: pouring molten lead into various orifices of their bodies; cutting their tongues out; pulling out their nails; ripping their skin off; sticking red-hot pokers into their eyes; tying their arms and legs to horses and literally tearing their bodies apart.

But, enjoyable as it was, converting the Marranos lost its charm after a while. So Torquemada got Ferdinand and Isabella to expel them all, thereby gutting the Spanish intelligentsia and dealing Spanish culture a blow from which it still hasn't recovered.

Well, enough of this. Back to the jokes.

(From a Spanish word meaning "pig.")

matza, matzo (MAHT-suh)

A flat cracker used particularly during Passover (when no leavened bread is allowed in the house) but also all year round. Matza commemorates the Hebrew's flight from Egypt, when there was no time to wait for bread to rise.

Matza is good with sweet (unsalted) butter. (So is just about everything else.)

matza ball (MAHT-suh BAWL)

A dumpling made from matza meal and used typically in a chicken broth to make matza ball soup.

Matza balls don't *have* to be heavy. I once made some following the recipe on a matza meal box, using good sweet butter instead of schmaltz, and when people ate them they rolled up their eyes so you could only see the whites, made a funny gurgling noise deep in their throats like they were coming, and shivered all over. I never did it again because I got tired of fighting off the marriage proposals.

As a name for a person, "matza ball" means "fatso."

matza brei (MAHT-suh BREI)

If there were any danger of the natural ingredients used

in matza brei ever running out, this entry wouldn't be here. You'd say "matza brei?" and I'd say "what?"

But since eggs are plentiful and the matza mines in Peru have a sufficient supply to meet present demand for another 1400 years (not to mention the fact that the Israelis have been experimenting with a method for synthesizing matzas out of sand), I don't suppose there's any harm in telling you how to make matza brei.

First you break some matzas (just regular matzas, not "egg, onion and styrofoam" or any other special kind) into little pieces. Then you beat eggs with a little water, and soak the matza pieces in it. Wait ten to fifteen minutes to give the matzas a chance to really sop up the liquid. Then sauté them in sweet butter over a low fire. Don't let them get dry; you want to keep them moist and juicy.

And there you have it—Jewish French toast. You can eat matza brei with jam, sour cream, applesauce, or melted butter and pepper.

In conclusion, I would say that matza brei is wonderful because it takes no special skill, and only a little practice, to make it perfectly, unlike many dishes that don't taste a tenth as good.

(Brei is the German word for "porridge.")

maven (MAY-vin)
An expert, a connoisseur.

maydala (MAY-duh-luh)
Young woman. Also, girl.
I think this is a really beautiful word. And I think that **shayna maydala** (qv) is a beautiful way to say "beautiful young woman."

mazel (MAH-zul)
Luck, fortune.
(Also see **goyisha mazel** and **yiddisha mazel**.)

mazel tov! (MAH-zuhl tuv)

Congratulations!

Literally, mazel tov means good luck, but in the sense of "(what) good fortune (you are having)!" not in the sense of "(I wish you) good luck!" So don't use it to mean good luck.

I don't actually know how you say good luck in Yiddish. Probably the assumption is that it's a futile gesture (see **yiddisha mazel**.)

mazuma (muh-ZOOM-uh)

Money, cash.

(From the Aramaic.)

mechaieh (see **makhaiya**)

meesa masheena (MEE-suh muh-SHEE-nuh)

A horrible death, as in the expressions *a meesa masheena af dir!* (uh MEE-suh muh-SHEE-nuh ahf deer)—a horrible death to you, and *nem arein a meesa masheena!* (nehm uh-REIN uh MEE-suh muh-SHEE-nuh)—take in a horrible death.

A. A. Roback suggests that masheena is the origin of the insulting name for a Jew, sheeny. This makes a lot of sense to me. If you imagine the typical situation, a goy would be abusing or beating up a Jew, or vice versa (somehow that seems less convincing, doesn't it?).

The Jew would be mad, and would be cursing at the goy. There's a good chance he'd be shouting "a meesa masheena af dir" or "nem arein a meesa masheena." To taunt him, the goy might shout it back: "m'sheena, m'sheeny." Thus Jews would come to be called sheenies, just as Italian- and Spanish-speakers came to be called spics because people teased them about the way they pronounced "speak."

Now if the angry Jew didn't shout "a meesa masheena,"

he'd probably shout *a moka af dir* (uh MAH-kuh ahf deer), a boil on you. This too would have been thrown back in his face until it became another abusive term for Jews, "mockie."

"Kike," however, seems to have a different origin. Older generations of Jews had an aversion to making an X, not only because the sign of the cross symbolized another religion, but because it was under that very sign that Jews had been tortured and murdered for centuries. So instead, they made a little circle, a *keikala*.

Leo Rosten suggests two situations in which Jews would have needed to make crosses (for which they would have substituted keikalas): as newly arrived immigrants filling out forms on Ellis Island, and as itinerant peddlers filling out order forms. Apparently miners in northeastern Pennsylvania referred to Jewish peddlers as "kike men," not intending any slur. (This reminds me of going to camp in Wisconsin in the mid-fifties and having the local people refer to the place, without a touch of malice, as "the Jew camp.")

megillah (muh-GIL-uh)
A whole long story. (Also see **Megillah** and **whole megillah**.)

Megillah (muh-GIL-uh)
The book read on Purim, which tells the story of Esther—in great detail. This led to the expression "the whole megillah," meaning a long, complicated story. (For the story itself, see **Purim**.)

There are actually five Megillahs; the Book of Ruth is one of them. But the word Megillah by itself always refers to the Book of Esther.

(From the Hebrew word for "scroll.")

mein kint (mein KINT)
My child.

melamed (muh-LAH-mud)
Hebrew teacher.

member of the tribe
A humorous way to refer to another Jew.

menorah (muh-NO- or NAW-ruh)
The special candleholder used on Chanukah.
Also, the candleholder used on the sabbath.
Shabbes menorahs hold seven candles; Chanukah menorahs hold nine—one for each night of the holiday plus the shamus (so called because it's used to light the others; see **shamus**).

mensch, menschlichkeit (mensh, MENSH-likh-keit)
This isn't going to be easy. Literally, mensch means a person, a human being. But it means much more than that.
To call someone a mensch is, in a certain way, the highest compliment you can pay them. It means they're mature, compassionate, decent, loving—everything a human being should be. **Menschlichkeit** means true humanity, real human dignity.
When mensch is used as the last word in a sentence, as it often is, it's always emphasized—"now *this* is a *mensch!*"—because there's little you can say beyond that.
Oriana Fallaci wrote a book called *A Man*. The feeling she wants to convey about this Greek patriot comes across even better in the Yiddish title *A Mensch*.
You don't have to be well known, or even exceptional (except in your menschlichkeit), to be a mensch, but the examples I'll give of mensches will be famous people, because otherwise you won't know who I'm talking about. Martin Luther King was a mensch. Albert Einstein was a mensch. Emma Goldman was a mensch. Salvador Allende was a mensch. Malcolm X was a mensch. Joan Baez is a mensch. Robert Redford is a mensch. And, if you ask me,

Abbie Hoffman is a mensch. (This is, needless to say, a partial—as well as a partisan—list.)

meshugga, meshuggina, meshugginer (muh-SHŎOG-uh, muh-SHŎOG-in-uh or -er)

A meshuggina is a woman who's meshugga. A meshugginer is a man who's meshugga.

Meshugga? That means, you know, fertoutst.

OK, OK, I'll define them. Don't get so excited.

A meshuggina is someone who would think this has been an adequate definition so far—you know, a crazy person. And meshugga means, of course, crazy.

Just to make things complicated, some people also use meshuggina to mean "crazy" and meshugga to mean "a crazy person."

Sometimes meshuggina is used affectionately: *And you thought that meant I didn't still love you? ... meshuggina!*

metsiah, mitsiah (met- or mit-SEE-yuh)

A bargain, a good deal.

Mostly used sarcastically to mean just the opposite, "a real prize." On *Your Show of Shows*, Sid Caesar had a Japanese houseboy called Taka Metsiah ("what a prize"). *You met her new husband? Taka metsiah!*

The sarcasm is often intensified by saying *a ganze metsiah*—a total bargain, a great deal.

(Metsiah means "a find" in Hebrew.)

mezuzah (muh-ZŎO-zuh)

A small, flat box, about one inch by three, which many Jews attach to their doorjambs to honor the Biblical commandment to inscribe the words of God "on the doorposts of thy house and upon thy gates."

The mezuzah is placed on the right side of the door, fairly high up, at a slant. Inside of it is a tiny scroll containing verses from Deuteronomy, beginning with the **shema**.

The use of the mezuzah goes back to the idea that God will protect a house marked with it, just as he passed over the houses of the Jews who marked their doors with lamb's blood when he killed the first-born sons in Egypt.

midrash; plural: midrashim (MID-rahsh, mid-rahsh-EEM)
A compilation of interpretations of the Bible made between about 2200 and 800 years ago.

Also, Jewish legends and folk literature, which are still being collected today.

mieskeit (MEES-keit)
Ugliness, ugly thing.

Older Jews who grew up in the shtetl sometimes use the expression *aza mieskeit*—"such ugliness!"—when referring to a little child, to fool the evil eye (see **kina hora**). This was done to a friend of mine when he was about five and he indignantly replied, "I'm not a mieskeit. I'm a zieskeit!" (a sweet thing).

mikvah (MIK-vuh)
A ritual bath used by married women seven days after the end of their periods, supposedly to purify themselves, and on certain other occasions.

Traditionally, husbands and wives were not allowed to have any physical contact (much less any sexual contact) while she was menstruating, or for a week afterward. Today only the most Orthodox Jews observe this custom.

milchedik, milchedika, milchik (MIL-khuh-dik, -dik-uh, MIL-khik)
Pertaining to foods that contain milk, butter, cheese, etc. and therefore may not be eaten at the same meal with meat. (See **kosher**.)

Also refers to the utensils used to prepare and eat such

foods, which may not be used with meat.

(Opposite: **flayshedik**. See **kosher** for details.)

minyan (MIN-yun)

The quorum (a minimum of ten men) required to hold a Jewish religious service. (Certain ceremonies, like weddings and brisses, are exempted.)

This requirement presumably derives from the deal Abraham struck with God that Sodom would not be destroyed if ten righteous men could be found in the city (better luck next time).

This seems to imply that as long as there's a Jewish service going on in your town, you're safe from earthquakes, hurricanes, tidal waves or whatever. So don't make the mistake Spain made; don't kick the Jews out. Every time they get a minyan together, they're protecting you from catastrophe.

mish-mosh (mish-mahsh, *not* mish-mash)

A mess, caused by several things (or kinds of things) being thrown together in disorder. For example, the political philosophies (if we can give them so grand a name) of most mainstream American public figures (if we can give *them* so grand a name) are mish-moshes of half-baked ideas, vague prejudices and the results of public opinion polls.

Mish-mosh also has a history as a non-Jewish expression (via German and Danish). This variant is pronounced mish-mash (as in hash), which sounds so goyish it sets my teeth on edge.

Mishnah (MISH-nuh)

A collection of commentaries on the Bible and laws covering everything from agriculture, marriage and divorce, civil suits and criminal offenses to religious practices and rituals. Compiled (in Hebrew) about 1800 years ago, the

Mishnah forms the older of the two parts of the Talmud (qv).

mishpawkha, mishbawkha (mish-PAW- or -BAW-khuh)
Family, in the sense of extended family, clan—not the little nuclear unit sitting around in the living room all wishing they were somewhere else (am I projecting?), but the whole, full-blown tribe.

mit
With.

mit fremde hent iz gut feier tsu sharen (mit FREM-duh HENT iz goŏt FEI-yur tsoo SHAH-ren)
It's good to poke the fire with somebody else's hand.

mit schlag (mit SHLAHG)
With whipped cream, as in *cafe mit schlag,* or hot strudel *mit schlag,* or strawberry shortcake *mit schlag,* or kiwi fruit and pear tart *mit schlag*—you get the idea.

mitsiah (see **metsiah**)

mitzvah (MITS-vuh)
Any one of the 613 commandments Jews are required to follow.

Since many of these command kindness to others, mitzvah has come to mean a good deed. One speaks of "doing a mitzvah" or "performing a mitzvah."

Some mitzvahs are fairly unusual. For example, it is a mitzvah to have sex (with your spouse, of course) on the sabbath—and for the pleasure of it, not just to have children. This is one of the less onerous duties imposed on Jews.

Some people are so good, they just seem unable to do

anything but mitzvahs. There's a wonderful story about one such, a woman so perfect in her life on earth that when she got to heaven, the angel at the gate said: "This is amazing. I've never seen anything like it. In your entire life, you've performed nothing but mitzvahs. Not one single sin! We can't let you into heaven like this. You have to be more like other people—flawed, prone to error. I'm going to send you back to earth for just three hours, and in that time, I want you to perform just one little sin. Remember now, Mrs. Zuckerman, a sin—no more mitzvahs."

Bewildered, Mrs. Zuckerman found herself back on Fairfax Avenue. It was around 10 P.M. on a Saturday night. She wandered into Canter's and saw a very unattractive old man sitting dejectedly at one of the tables. An idea came into her head.

"Excuse me, mister," she said, "may I join you?"

One thing led to another and by midnight she was in the old man's bed. As 1 A.M. approached, she got up quietly, slipped into her clothes and stood anxiously awaiting her ascent into heaven. Just then, from the bed, came the old man's sigh: "Oy, Mrs. Zuckerman, what a mitzvah you performed tonight!"

mogen david (MAW-gun DUH or DAY-vid)
The six-pointed star of David, a relatively recent Jewish symbol (only 700 or 800 years old).

momzer, mumzer (MAHM-, MAWM- or MUM-zer)
A bastard, in both senses; that is, an illegitimate child or . . . you know . . . a bastard.
(From the Hebrew).

M.O.T.
Member of the tribe; that is, a Jew.

mother (Jewish)
I don't personally believe that Jewish mothers are all that

mitzvah

different from other kinds of mothers. For one thing, my mother was nothing like the stereotype (she used to abandon me on our cabin floor for days at a time when she went out deer hunting). For another thing, lots of non-Jewish mothers *are* just like the stereotype (all Italian mothers, for example).

But it's worth keeping the "Jewish mother" myth alive, if only for the jokes. Now I don't mean run-of-the-mill jokes like the one about the psychiatrist who tells a Jewish mother that her son has an Oedipus complex. ("Oedipus, shmoedipus," she answers, "just so long as he loves his mother.") Or the one about how many Jewish mothers it takes to change a lightbulb. (None at all. "Don't give it a moment's thought. I'll be perfectly fine here in the dark. I'll just sit and think about you.")

No, I mean the truly extraordinary, *outré* jokes like this one:

A guy is madly in love with a woman. He tells her he'll do anything to prove he loves her.

So the woman says: "I think the problem is your mother. She's always guilt-tripping you with that smothering, phony "concern" of hers. If you really want to prove you love me, *cut your mother's heart out and bring it to me.*"

Well, the guy can't believe his ears. Murder his loving, devoted mother, whose only thought has always been for his well-being!! It's unthinkable!

But eventually, his desperate love for the woman wins out. One evening, when his mother is serving him a bowl of chicken soup, he whirls around and stabs her with a breadknife. He cuts out her heart and stumbles off with it in his hand. But halfway to the door, blinded by his tears, he trips and falls, dropping the heart.

From the floor, the heart says: "Did you hurt yourself?"

motza, motzo (see **matza**)

moyl

The man who circumcises baby boys at a briss (qv).

The standard joke about moyls is that although they don't make much money, they get a lot of tips.

There's also a good one about a man who passes by a store window with nothing in it but a beautiful antique clock. He goes in and says, "Excuse me, do you repair Seth Thomas wall clocks?"

The man in the shop says, "I don't repair any kind of clock. I'm a moyl."

"But in your window you have a clock."

"And what would *you* put in the window?"

mumzer (see **momzer**)

N

naches (see **nakhes**)

nafka (NAHF-kuh)
Whore.
Kiki, you nafka you, I'll give it all up for you! (Lenny Bruce, "Father Flotsky's Triumph").
(From the Aramaic for "streetwalker.")

nakhes (NAH-khuhs)
Joyful gratification in the accomplishments of another.
Nakhes is what you get from your son being a doctor.
(Also see **goyim nakhes** and **kvell**.)
(Nakhes is Hebrew for "contentment.")

nar (nahr)
A fool.

narishkeit (NAHR-ish-keit)
Foolishness.

nayfish (NAY-fish)
A poor soul.
(Also see **shlemiel**.)

N.D.G.
Short for **nem dos gelt**—take the money (and work out the details later).

nebbish (NEH-bish)

A nothing, a nobody. The sort of person who, when he enters a room, creates the impression that someone has just left.

(Also see **shlemiel**.)

-nik

This Slavic suffix converts any word into a name for a devotee of whatever that word refers to. Now that's crystal clear, isn't it? It's easier with examples: Someone who's beat is a beatnik; someone involved in the antiwar movement is a peacenik; someone who noudges all the time is a nudnik (originally, "noudge-nik.")

-nik got more popular in the United States after the Russians launched Sputnik in 1957, but it was widely used by Jews and Slavs long before that. In Slavic countries, -nik doesn't have the cute, trivializing connotation it does in the United States today. For example, in nineteenth-century Russia, there was a movement of populists who tried to incite the peasants into a revolt against the tsar. They were called *narodniks* (after *narod*, the word for "people").

nisht lozen zikh onton a yokh iz gringer vie es arunter tsuvarfen (nisht LAWZ-un zeekh AWN-tun ah YAWKH iz GRIN-ger vee es uh-RŎON-ter tsoo-VARF-un)

It's easier never to let them put a yoke on you, than it is to throw one off.

no khoupie, no shtupie (no KHŎOP-ee, no SHTŎOP-ee)

The Jewish princess' equivalent to "no tickee, no washee."

It means "no sex unless we're married." Literally, "no wedding canopy, no fuck-ee." (See **khoupa** and **shtup**.)

noch (nawkh)

1. More; too.

Noch gelt vil er! (NAWKH GELT vil ayr)—he wants money too! (His name in print isn't enough?)

2. There! (said when you hit someone).

nosh (nahsh)
To snack.
Also, a snack.

nosherei (nahsh-uh-REI)
The kind of stuff you normally nosh on—potato chips, peanuts, cookies, candy. Nosherei is usually chazerei, but it doesn't have to be; a bowl of grapes, salami, cheese or, for that matter, any kind of hors d'oeuvre, all qualify as nosherei.

noudge (noŏj)
This, for me, is the archetypical Jewish word. If I had to give you the flavor of Yiddish while standing on one foot, I would teach you this one word.

It means to pester, to nag, to bother, to annoy. A noudge is someone who noudges. Someone a goy might describe as "pushy," a Jew would call a noudge. Noudge is commonly heard in the expression: *stop being such a noudge!*

There's a wonderful story about two brothers. One was easygoing and thoughtless, and completely irreligious. But he was also incredibly lucky, and in fact, had grown quite rich as the result of a long series of lucky breaks. The other brother was dutiful and punctilious to a fault; he never forgot a religious duty. Yet his luck was wretched, and he was quite poor.

One day when the pious brother was in shul, he decided, like Job, to ask God what justice there was in his condition. "Oh, Lord," he said, "why is it that my brother, who never goes to shul, who never performs a mitzvah, is rich and happy, while I am a miserable pauper? Every morning I pray to you for an hour. Every holiday, I spend all day in shul dovening. Before every important decision, I beseech your guidance. You are always in my thoughts. And all day long, your name is on my lips. Oh, Lord, why have you cursed me with such bad luck?"

A crash of thunder shook the shul, and God's voice roared from on high: "Because you're such a noudge!"

novy, nova (NO-vee, NO-vuh)

A kind of lox that comes from Nova Scotia. Novy costs more than other kinds of lox, and is only very lightly salted. It's supposed to have a more delicate flavor.

I say, "supposed to" because I personally can't stand lox. Yes, that's right, a Jew who can't *stand* lox. So just throw your racial stereotypes out the window—I don't like lox, my hair is straight and blond, my eyes are blue, I'm a terrible businessman, I can't read, and I have an IQ of 43.

Actually, not *all* that is true. My eyes are brown, and I do like lox.

nu (noo)

Nu?

Oh, you want a definition. Nu, so I'll give you a definition. Nu means "well" or "so."

One of the most common uses is when someone is coming back from finding something out. They come in the door, and you say, "Nu?" (So, what did you find out?).

Another common use is when you ask someone a question and they take some time thinking of what to answer. If you get impatient, you say, "Nu?" (Well?). Thus nu would be the perfect word to use on game shows. When the contestant's ten seconds are up, the host would say, "Nu?"

I'm having a hard time explaining the different nuances of nu because they depend so much on tone. (In fact, the word "nuances" itself originally meant (in Old French) "shades of meaning of the word 'nu.'")

For example, if you're helping a four-year-old read a book and she's had a few moments to think about a hint you gave her about a word she's stuck on, you say it like this: "Nu?" But if you're waiting for your sixteen-year-old son to explain why he pawned your good silver and ran away with the maid and gambled away all the money and is calling you collect from Atlantic City to send him bus fare home, you say it like this: "Nu?" See what I mean?

To be perfectly honest, you can almost always substitute "well" or "so" for "nu." Nu just has a better flavor. It's like the difference between that cheese stuff you squirt out of a nozzle, and schmaltz with gribbenes.

Here's a joke with nu:

A man goes to Rabinowitz, the tailor, and orders a pair of pants. Six weeks later they still aren't ready.

"Rabinowitz!" he says, "what can possibly be taking you so long? Six weeks for a pair of pants! It took God only six *days* to create the entire universe."

"Nu, look at it."

nudnik (NŎŎD-nik)

A pest, a bore. Someone who's a nuisance because he's such a jerk. (Literally, a "noudge-nik.")

A man goes to a psychiatrist. The psychiatrist says, "What seems to be the trouble?"

(This is a very sensitive psychiatrist who knows that in a psychiatrist joke, the psychiatrist always has to ask, "What seems to be the trouble?" It wouldn't really be a psychiatrist joke without that line, and this psychiatrist is a good guy, he doesn't want to screw up my joke, so he says, "What seems to be the trouble?"

(But if this were a real session, with a real person, and not just a character in a joke coming to him for help, he would have said "What the fuck's wrong with you? You look terrible!" because his technique is very confrontational. He believes in shocking people out of their complacency, jarring them so badly that they just start babbling whatever's in their mind without censoring it the way they usually do.

(In this way, he's like the shrink played by James Earl Jones in *End of the Road* (a very underrated movie, in my opinion. The cinematography alone makes it worth seeing, not to mention Jones' and Stacy Keach's performances and John Barth's story.))

(Anyway, this psychiatrist is flexible enough to break free from his normal way of operating and say, just like the psychiatrist in any other joke, "What seems to be the trouble?")

The guy answers, "I don't know what to do, Doc. I keep talking to myself all day long."

"Well, now, that's not so serious," the psychiatrist says soothingly. "Lots of people do that."

"Yeah but Doctor, you don't know what a nudnik I am."

O

omayn (oh- or aw-MAYN)
1. Amen.
2. True; right.

ongepachkit (see **ungepachkit**)

orim zein iz kayn shanda, ober es iz oykh nisht kayn grosser koved (AW-rim zein iz kayn SHAHN-duh, OH-bayr es iz OYKH nisht kayn GROH-ser KAW-ved)

Being poor is no disgrace, but it's not a great honor either.

Orthodox
The most traditional of the three Jewish religious denominations. See **Reform** for more details.

oy
Oh.

oysvorf (OYS-vurf)
A bum; an outcast.
Some weird oysvorf I caught wearing girl's panties (William Styron, *Sophie's Choice*).

oy vay; oy vay iz mir (oy VAY, oy VAY iz MEER)
Oh, woe (sometimes, "oh, no!" is a better translation); oh, woe is me.

P

the Pale (payl)

The twenty-five provinces of Tsarist Russia outside of which Jews needed special permission to live. The Pale was established in 1772 and abolished by the Communists in 1917. (Also known as **the Pale of Settlement**.)

The expression "beyond the Pale," meaning beyond hope or help, refers not to the Jewish Pale but to the Irish Pale, the area controlled by the English in medieval Ireland.

pareve (PAH-ruh-vuh)

Neither meat nor dairy and thus OK to eat with either. (See **kosher** for details.)

paskudnyak, paskudnik (pahs-kood-NYAK or -NIK)

A disgusting person.

Passover (PAS-oh-vur)

The holiday that celebrates the Hebrews' escape from slavery in Egypt. It's celebrated for eight days (seven in Israel and by Reform Jews), and a feast called a seder is held on the first (and sometimes the second) night. The Haggadah is read at the seder, and special foods are eaten.

No leavened bread (khometz) is allowed in the house during Passover; matza is eaten instead. This is to remind Jews of the haste with which the Hebrews fled Egypt, without time to even wait for their bread to rise. Special foods are eaten: bitter herbs, as a reminder of the bitterness of slavery; and kharosis (qv), as a reminder of the mortar which the Hebrews used in building the pyramids.

The seder begins when the leader of the service holds up a tray with three matzas on it and says, "This is the bread of affliction that our fathers ate in the land of Egypt." Later in the seder, the youngest child who can handle the four questions in Hebrew asks them. They begin: *mah nishtana hulaila huzeh*—"how is this night different from all other nights?"

Actually, Passover shadows a much older holiday, common to all agricultural cultures—the spring planting festival. This is also true of Easter, where the symbolism is even clearer. You bury something (a seed) in the ground and after some time, it is reborn (as a plant).

And just as Passover is a Judaized planting festival, so Easter is a Christianized Passover. In fact, the Last Supper was a seder.

(Also see **khometz** and **mah nishtana**.)

pastrami (puh-STRAH-mee)
Highly spiced smoked beef.

Roumanian pastrami is the best, and Bernstein's-on-Essex-Street in New York has the best Roumanian pastrami. (They also serve kosher Chinese food.)

It was in Bernstein's that I was served by a Chinese waiter who spoke fluent Yiddish. I didn't want to embarrass him by asking about it, but as I was leaving I said to the cashier, "Tell me, where did that Chinese waiter learn to speak Yiddish so well?"

"Shhh!" whispered the cashier. "He thinks we're teaching him English."

payess (PAY-yus)
Earlocks—that is, the ringlets that will grow from the

point where a man's sideburns meet his hairline, if he doesn't trim them.

In observance of the commandment, "you shall not clip your hair at the temples or mar the edges of your beard," devout Jews do let them grow, at least long enough to reach their earlobes and sometimes much longer.

Pesach (PAY-sahkh)
Passover (qv).
(Hebrew for "to pass over," "to spare.")

pesadika (PAY-suh-dik-uh)
Kosher for Pesach—that is, containing no leavening, or otherwise blessed for the holiday.

There seems to be quite a racket going on here, blessing all kinds of things that couldn't in a million years have leavening in them, so they can get the little seal, so observant Jews will buy them during the Passover season.

(See **khometz** for more on this scandal, which threatens to tear Judaism apart.)

petzel, petzula (PEHTS-ul, PETZS-ul-uh)
Diminutives of putz (qv).

Ph.G.
Papa hot gelt (PAH-puh HAHT GELT)—Daddy has money (the degree to look for if you're going to college to get married).

pisher (PISH-ur)
Someone inconsequential, usually because s/he is so young. Almost always used with "you little": *Why, you little pisher!* (Literally, "pïsser.")

The English expression "little squirt" captures the figurative meaning and also hints at the literal one.

pisk

A not-very-refined word for mouth.

Also, figuratively, a loudmouth.

Oy, hot er a pisk! (OY, haht EHR ah PISK)—Boy, does he have a mouth!

plotke-macher (PLAWT-kuh MAH-kher)

A conniving gossip.

(From a Slavic word for "gossip" + German "maker.")

plotz (plahts)

To explode.

Stop! Please!! If I laugh anymore, I'll plotz. (Laughter seems to be the main thing that creates the risk of plotzing.)

I always thought plotz meant "to collapse," and I've heard it used that way by other people too: *I'm so tired I could plotz*, or *if I have to stay on my feet for another second I'm going to plotz.*

Plotz may be one of those words whose meaning was guessed at by younger generations of non-Yiddish-speaking Jews until it finally took on the new, guessed-at sense. When you hear someone talk about laughing so hard they could plotz, and you don't know the word, "collapse" seems the most likely meaning.

A lot of young Jews who know little or no Yiddish feel that they *should* (and therefore that they do). I know I often assumed I knew what a word meant because I'd heard it used many times, but when I found out what it actually meant, I discovered my guess had been completely wrong. For example, it wasn't too long ago that I discovered that **shlemiel** and **shlimazl** don't mean the same thing, and that's really square-one, Baltic-and-Mediterranean Yiddish (I refer, of course, to the dark-purple monopoly, not the European seas).

In *Soon to Be a Major Motion Picture*, Abbie Hoffman

111

writes that at one point during the Chicago Seven trial he accused Judge Hoffman of being a *shanda fur die goyim*. He translates this as meaning "a front man for the goyim" when actually it means to make "a scandal in front of the goyim," to embarrass all Jews by acting in some shameful way someplace where the goyim can see you.

If my experience is any indication, a lot of the Yiddish you hear from younger Jews is the result of this kind of guessing at the meaning of words. (After all, you don't want to ask your *parents*. They might take it as a sign of interest in Jewish culture and start telling you stories about life in Poland. It could be a disaster. Better to guess. So what if you guess wrong? No one will know.)

pogrom (puh-GRAWM)

What Russian and Polish and Ukrainian peasants did for sport before bowling was invented—namely to go out and beat the shit out of every Jew they could find (except of course for the women, whom they raped), to loot their houses and then burn the village down and, if it was Christmas, or if they just happened to be in the mood, to kill them all.

Wasn't it fun learning what "pogrom" means?

(Pogrom is Russian, and means "like thunder.")

ponim (see **punim**)

potch (pahch)

A slap, usually on the tokhis (ass). *Oy, I'm going to give you such a potch!*

Potch and frosk refer to relatively mild blows. Frosk is somewhat stronger than potch only because it's more likely to be to the face, and therefore to hurt more, than a *potch in tokhis*. A klop is stronger than either—it can knock you

112

unconscious. A frosk can really hurt, and about the most a potch can do is sting.

There's a Jewish saying that's just the opposite of "sticks and stones can break my bones, but names will never hurt me": *a potch fergeht, un a vort beshteht* (ah PAHCH fer-GAYT awn ah VAWRT buh-SHTAYT)—a slap goes away, but a word stays.

potchky, potchky around (PAHCH-kee)
To fuss, to futz, to fool around with.
Paulie, stop potchkying around with that chemistry set and come eat your dinner.

psssh!
Fantastic! Wonderful!

punim, ponim (POŎ-, POO- or PAW-nim)
Face.
Much is said in praise of goyisha punims, with their freckles and little turned-up noses. But I'm a fan of the dark, sloe-eyed, intense, Semitic look myself.

pupik (POŎ-pik)
Bellybutton.
Don't confuse **pupik** with **punim** (although it does present some kinky possibilities).
Pupik can also mean the gizzard of a bird.

Purim (POO-rim)
A Jewish holiday, occurring in the early spring, which celebrates the victory of Persian Jews over Haman, who was the chief counselor to King Ahasuerus (possibly Artaxerxes II, if the Purim story has any historical validity).
Haman wanted to kill all the Jews, making this an old

Oy, such a punim!

story in more ways than one. Queen Esther was Jewish, but the king didn't know that. Esther's uncle Mordecai was one of Haman's prime targets. So Esther said to King Ahasuerus, "Someone is plotting to kill me."

"Just tell me who it is," said the king, "and he'll never know what hit him" (or words to that effect—you understand that we don't have the exact dialogue; this was thousands of years ago. We have to use our judgment in recreating what it would have sounded like. So don't give me a hard time about it, OK?).

"Haman," Esther said.

"Haman?!" said King Ahasuerus.

"Well," said Esther, "he's planning to kill all the Jews, and that includes me."

"Holy moly," thought the king, "beautiful Esther, my favorite wife? This Haman is some sort of deranged Dr. Strangelove. I haven't been so badly advised since I fired Kissinger." And he had Haman hanged on the very same gallows Haman had prepared for Mordecai.

(That "very same gallows" bit is stretching it, if you ask me. I mean, they don't even know which king it was; how are they going to keep track of which gallows was which in Persepolis 2300 years ago? Sounds to me like a little something to keep the kids bright-eyed in Sunday school).

So, that's the story. By telling it to you in my inimitably breezy and succinct manner, I've saved you from having to listen to the whole Megillah, since that's what the Book of Esther, read on Purim, is called (and it *is* a whole megillah).

By the way, did you know that Henry Kissinger was actually the model for Dr. Strangelove in the movie? (This was before he got famous.) In fact, the film makers were worried that Kissinger would recognize himself and sue them for libel. Now that I've told you that, it's obvious, isn't it? We can even see his behavior from 1964 on as an example of life imitating art.

Anyway, on Purim you eat hamentashen (qv), make an ungodly racket with gregors (qv), feast, dance, wear costumes, and distribute gifts to the poor.

pushka, pushkie (PŎOSH-kuh or -kee)
A small box, usually made of metal, to collect contributions for some charitable organization. Some people keep pushkas in their homes, and you see them on the checkout counters of many small stores in Jewish neighborhoods.

putz (puhts)
Putz originally meant "penis," but now it's almost always

used figuratively, as in *Who is that putz?*

Putz is stronger and more hostile than "schmuck." You might say to a friend: *you schmuck!* in the spirit of friendly (although exasperated) criticism, but if you say: *you putz!* it probably means you're thinking twice about the friendship.

(Also see **schmuck, shlong** and **shvantz**.)

Q

question

Why do Jews always answer a question with another question?

Why not? Why shouldn't they? There's something wrong maybe with answering a question with another question? This is the most important thing you have to worry about? Children are starving in India and all you can think about is why Jews answer a question with another question? This by you is problem? Are you kidding?

You had enough?

R

rabbi (RA-bei)

In twentieth-century America, the Jewish equivalent of a Protestant minister—that is, the person who leads religious services, counsels members of the congregation on personal and religious problems, officiates at ceremonies, visits the sick, preaches sermons, supervises the Sunday school, etc. This combination of duties is new to Judaism.

Traditionally, the rabbi (**rebbe** or **rov** in Yiddish) was a teacher and interpreter of the Torah and Talmud. (Literally, "rabbi" means "teacher.") Rabbis were not ordained, and they rarely led religious services (usually the cantor did, but any learned member of the congregation could). They held no power or authority other than what grew out of respect for their learning and wisdom.

Rov is the more formal Yiddish word, and is used particularly to refer to the modern-day, ordained rabbi. **Rebbe** is the more affectionate term. Rebbe could refer to someone who was no more than the teacher of a handful of boys.

The leaders of Chassidic sects are always called rebbes, never rovs. Chassidic rebbes differ from other rabbis in several ways: they are treated with more veneration by their followers; some inherit, rather than earn, the title; and some have been said to work miracles. So Jesus Christ was more like a Chassidic rebbe than a conventional rabbi.

The closest present-day equivalent to a traditional rabbi is a judge. In fact the judgment of Solomon—where two women argue over who's the mother of a child, and the king says cut him in two and let them each have half, and the real mother says: oh, no, let her have him—is the kind of story you hear about famous rabbis (and probably would be a story about a famous rabbi if Solomon hadn't gotten there first).

Rabbis were expected to know the laws embodied in the Talmud and other sacred writings intimately, and to apply them wisely. But of course that wasn't always the case. (I feel a joke coming on.)

A traveling peddler finds himself in a small shtetl (eastern European village) on a Friday night. After shul he begins to trudge off down the main street, but a man calls after him, "Wait, stranger, where are you going? It's the sabbath. Come to my house, have dinner with us, spend the night."

The peddler is delighted, and even more delighted by the superb meal and comfortable bed. In the morning, over a huge breakfast, he turns to his host and says, "This has been one of the nicest times of my life. How can I ever thank you?"

"Just take care of this," his host says, handing him a detailed bill for each item he ate, the towel and bedsheets he used, etc.

The peddler is flabbergasted. "Are you crazy?" he says. "You *invited* me here! I was your *guest!* Not to mention that hospitality to strangers on shabbes is a mitzvah, a sacred duty."

"Look," says his host, "there's no sense in arguing. Let's just go to the rabbi and put the whole dispute before him."

"Yes, yes, let's do that!" cries the enraged peddler. "I'd love to hear what a rabbi will say to the idea of charging a shabbes guest!"

So off they go to the rabbi. The peddler, fuming with indignation, tells his side of the story. When the rabbi turns to the host, he smiles pleasantly and says, "There's no disagreement about the facts. It's just the way this stranger told it."

"Well," says the rabbi, stroking his beard, "this is certainly an unusual case. But based on my many years of study of the Talmud, I must say that the decision is clear. The bill must be paid."

The peddler can hardly believe his ears. And yet this is a rabbi, and the rabbi has decided.

As they leave the rabbi's house, the peddler takes his purse from his pocket and begins counting out the money he owes.

"What are you doing?" asks the host.

"What do you mean, what am I doing?" says the peddler. "I'm paying you your money."

"*Paying* me?" says the host. "For my hospitality to a shabbes guest. Don't be silly!"

"But you *asked* for the money! You gave me a *bill!*"

"Oh, that!" laughs the host. "That was just to show you what a dope our rabbi is."

rakhmones (rahkh-MAWN-is)
Compassion, empathy. Not your thin-blooded, abstract, Christian pity, but real, sloppy, emotional caring for people.
The best example of rakhmones I know of is Toni Morrison's book, *The Bluest Eye*.

reb
Mister. (Don't confuse this with **rebbe**.)

rebbe (REH-bee)
Rabbi.
Or teacher (see **rabbi**).

rebitsin (REH-bit-sin)
Although this word means "rabbi's wife," it always makes

me think of a little rabbit. As a result, whenever a rabbi's wife does, in fact, somewhat resemble a rabbit—say by having buck teeth, or a frenzied manner, or a nose that crinkles when she talks—it always seems appropriate to me on some deep level.

Reform

The most liberal of the three Jewish religious denominations, the other two being Orthodox and Conservative.

Orthodox Judaism is the traditional practice, with full observance of dietary restrictions and other ritual requirements. Reform Judaism rose up in opposition to it in nineteenth-century Germany. It seeks to distill the ethical spirit of Judaism while discarding most of the specific laws. (You won't be far off if you think of it as sort of a Jewish Unitarianism.) Conservative Judaism, the most recent movement, attempts a compromise between Reform and Orthodox.

There's a famous joke about how the three denominations are different:

A boy keeps nagging his mother to get him a Christmas tree like all the other kids on the block. At last she gives in, but to take the curse off her decision, she goes to an Orthodox rabbi and asks him if he will consent to say a brawkha (blessing) over the tree. He turns beet red and orders her out of the shul.

Next she goes to a Conservative rabbi, who says he'd like to help her out, but just can't bring himself to say a brawkha over a Christmas tree.

Finally she goes to a Reform rabbi. "My dear lady," he says, "I'd be glad to. Just tell me one thing: what's a brawkha?"

Rosh Hashonah (properly: RAWSH hah-SHAW-nuh; commonly: RUSH huh-SHUH-nuh)

The Jewish New Year holiday, which comes in the early

(see **Reform**)

fall. With Yom Kippur, one of the two high holidays.
(Also see **l'shona tova** and **shofer**.)

rov (rawv, ruhv)
Rabbi (qv).

rugelach (RŎO-guh-lakh)
Crescent-shaped cookies dusted with sugar.

S

saykhel (SAY-khul)

Common sense; smarts.

Freg an aytsa yenem, un hob dayn saykhel bei dir (FRAYG ahn AYT-suh YAYN-um, un hahb dayn SAY-khul bei DEER)—ask for advice, then use your own head.

SCH

See **SH** for all SCH entries, except for the few below:

schlag (see **mit schlag**)

schlock; adjectives: **schlock, schlocky** or **schlock-house** (qv) (shlahk, SHLAHK-ee)

Poorly made, shoddy.

Also, things that are poorly made. *Sure he'll give you a deal. On schlock like that, he ought to give you a deal.*

schlock-house (SHLAHK-hows)

A place that sells schlock, but more commonly used as an adjective. *I wouldn't sell that schlock-house merchandise to my worst enemy.*

schlockmeister (SHLAHK-meis-ter)

Someone who sells (or is otherwise involved with) junk. (Literally, "schlock master.")

schmaltz (shmahlts, shmawlts)

Literally, melted animal fat, typically chicken fat, which is used extensively in Jewish cooking. (See **chopped liver** and **gribbenes**.)

Since schmaltz can be smeared on bread, and since it's usually laid on thick, the word came to mean laying the drama, the sentimentality, on thick—first in theatrical circles and then elsewhere. In this sense, there is the adjective, **schmaltzy**, and the verb, to **schmaltz** (something) **up**.

schmuck (shmuhk)

A prick, in both the literal and figurative senses. That is: a penis, or a person you don't like.

A schmuck can also be a dope, as in: *so you, schmuck, you believed him!*

Sometimes the two meanings of schmuck are played against each other, as in this joke:

Mr. Levy, a widower, retires to Miami Beach. Being a shy sort, and not knowing anyone there, he has a lonely time of it. Every day he sits and stares out into the water.

Another man about his age usually sits near him on the beach. This guy is always in the middle of a large crowd of people, telling jokes and laughing.

Finally Levy gets up the courage to speak to him:

"Excuse me, mister, but you seem to have a knack for meeting people. No one pays any attention to me. Can you give me some advice on what I can do about it?"

"Sure," says the man. "The first step is getting noticed. Now, how can we make people notice you? Hmmmm...I've got it! The circus is in town this week. Go down there and rent a camel. Ride up and down Collins Avenue on it for a couple of days. Everybody who sees you will wonder, 'who is that man?' Soon you'll be recognized everywhere you go, and you'll have more friends than you know what to do with."

This seems like a slightly bizarre plan to Mr. Levy, but he doesn't have any better idea, so he goes and rents the camel, puts on a safari jacket, Bermuda shorts and a pith helmet, and rides up and down Collins Avenue.

The next morning, when he arrives in the garage of his hotel to get back on the camel, he discovers that it's been stolen and immediately calls the police.

"A camel?!" says the policeman on the phone. "Well, I guess I'll just make a report out like on a car. What color was it?"

"I don't know," Levy says. "Camel-colored, I guess."

"Did it have one hump or two?"

"Who can remember details like that?" Levy asks in exasperation. "One hump. No, wait...two...no...I think it had one hump."

"Was it male or female?" the policeman asks.

"I don't know! How can you expect me . . . Wait a minute. It was a male."

"You sure about that?" asks the cop.

"Positive," Levy says.

"Look, mister, how can you be so sure what sex your camel was when you can't even remember how many humps it had or what color it was?"

"Well, it just occurred to me—as I was riding along Collins Avenue, people kept pointing and saying, 'Look at that schmuck on that camel.'"

(Also see **putz, shlong, shvantz** and **schlemiel**.)

(In German, "schmuck" means "ornament," "jewelry." So its figurative use is similar in origin to the English expression "the family jewels.")

schnaps (shnahps)

Whiskey; sometimes also refers to brandy or other hard liquor.

(What do Jews know about drinking? There's hard liquor—schnaps—and sickly sweet red wine, and that's it. Even beer is a slightly exotic, goyisha drink.

Now if there were sections in the Talmud devoted to the differences between ouzo and raki, or which is better, the cabernet or the zinfandel grape? . . . ah, *then* Jews would know all about liquor.)

seder (SAY-dur)

The special meal and ceremony held on the first night (or the first two nights) of Passover (qv).

Sephardim; adjective: **Sephardic** (suh-PHAHR-dim or -deem; suh-PHAHR-dik)

Jews from Spain, Portugal, North Africa and other Mediterranean countries, as opposed to **Ashkenazim** (qv).

For some reason, the people who standardize (or, rather,

attempt to standardize) the spelling of Hebrew words in English have gotten it into their collective little head that the Sephardic way of pronouncing these words is closer to the original. So when s appears at the end of the word, they change it to **th**.

Now I don't have anything against Sephardic Jews—some of my best friends are Sephardic Jews—but almost all American and European Jews are Ashkenazim. So the words are pronounced Ashkenazic but spelled Sephardic. You read Shavuoth, but say Shavuos. You read Succoth, but say Succos.

Sometimes the pronunciation comes to follow the Sephardic spelling, as in the name of a temple or hospital—Beth Israel, say. "Beth" is really "bes," which means "house of," as in bes midrash—house of study, synagog. You can see how confusing this would be if, for example, you saw Beth and Bess standing in front of a bes midrash called Beth Israel.

And anyway, the **th** has nothing to do with what Hebrew sounded like originally. It comes from the lisp that makes Spaniards from Castile pronounce their language wrong.

I don't know why I get so upset about it, but I just think words should be spelled the way they sound instead of trying to suck around the Sephardic Jews. So what if they're more Semitic than the rest of us? What's so wonderful about being short and dark and having curly black hair all over your body?

And *none* of my best friends are Sephardic Jews, because they're as rare as hens' teeth, and the ones that *are* around all have names like Luzzatti and Pappo that make you think they're Italian or something. And they all *look* Italian too. And they're always talking about Spinoza. Big deal, Spinoza—the one famous Sephardic Jew. What about the great Ashkenazic Jews like Einstein...Freud...Maxie Baer?

Oh, I shouldn't let it bother me, I gueth. Ha! Pretty

annoying, ithn't it? Oh, yeth, after a while it can really begin to pith you off.

(Also see **Ladino**.)

Einstein　　　**Freud**　　　**Baer**

shabbes (SHAH-bus)

The Jewish sabbath, which lasts from sunset Friday till sunset Saturday.

(Also see **shabbes goy**.)

shabbes goy (SHAH-bus goy)

A non-Jew hired, typically by a shul, to perform the tasks Jews are forbidden to do on the sabbath, like turn lights on and off. The reasoning (if we can call it that) goes like this: Jews are forbidden to work on the sabbath. Building a fire is work. (Of course, so is freezing to death, but anyway . . .)

Turning on an electric light is equivalent to making a fire—it's somewhere right around here that we begin to leave the realm of reason. An electric light is similar to a fire in that it provides light, but turning one on is very easy while making a fire is hard. Since we're supposed to be avoiding work, not light bulbs, it would seem that God's commandment would be better followed by sitting back in an easy chair and watching television on the sabbath, but ah!—television works by electricity, electricity is like fire, making fire is work, so turning on a television set is forbidden.

Maybe the rabbis who wrote the Talmud lived in houses with inadequate wiring—one 15-amp fuse for the whole place, lots of extension cords crammed into one socket, like those pictures they always showed us during Fire Prevention Week—so it seemed perfectly reasonable to them to equate electricity and fire. But this still doesn't let them off the hook, since even if electricity is likely to *cause* fire, turning on an electric light, unlike building a fire, still isn't work.

Some recently excavated murals seem to indicate that Babylonian light switches were extremely hard to flick. Servants are being pictured using both hands and more or less leaning into the task with one leg in front of the other. This might begin to explain things.

Anyway, Orthodox Jews in the shtetl would hire shabbes goys to light the lamps in the shul, to turn their television sets on and off, and so on.

But wait, I almost forgot the *most* irrational part. Elevators work by electricity, right? Electricity = fire = work, right? Therefore, you can't use elevators on shabbes. So if you want to visit someone on the fourteenth floor, you have to walk up the stairs! God forbid you should work on the sabbath.

Also, cars run by spark plugs and spark plugs make fire and therefore you can't use cars (or buses) on shabbes. So if you want to go somewhere five miles away, you have to walk. God forbid you should work on the sabbath. Trains—they work directly on electricity, or by steam created by coal fires—either way, fire = work, no good on shabbes.

And it gets *worse*. Electric vibrators, for example. Now if there's anything that shouldn't be classified as work . . .

shabbes

shacher-macher (SHAHKH-ur MAHKH-ur)

A finagler; a wheeler-dealer.

shadkhen (SHAHD-khun)

A matchmaker.

Sometimes a pun is made with "shotgun," another kind of matchmaker.

Shadkhens have some advantages over other ways to meet a mate, as the following joke demonstrates:

Desperate because her thirty-year-old daughter Sharon was still not married, Mrs. Katz secretly placed an ad for her in the personals column of the newspaper:

Lovely Jewish girl, refined, excellent cook, seeks to meet mature, established Jewish gentleman. Object: matrimony. Box 512.

When Sharon found out about this, she was livid, but eventually Mrs. Katz was able to convince her that no one would know who placed the ad, and maybe some good would come of it. In fact, as the days went by, Sharon got more and more enthusiastic about the idea. Finally a reply to the ad was delivered from the newspaper.

Sharon tore open the envelope, read the letter, and burst into tears. "Sharon, sweetie, what's wrong!" cried her mother.

In a choked voice, Sharon gasped, "It's from papa!"

shah!

Quiet! Shh!

shalom (shuh-LOHM; traditionally in Yiddish, SHO-lum or SHAW-lum)
1. Peace.
2. Hello.
3. Goodbye.

shalom aleichem (SHO-lum, SHAW-lum or shuh-LOHM uh-LAY-khim)

Peace be with you. The traditional way for Jews to greet and say goodbye to each other. (This obviously goes back a long way, since Arab Muslims say virtually the same thing: salaam alaykum.)

The appropriate response is **aleichem shalom** ("and unto you, peace").

shamus

When pronounced SHAH-mis, the word is usually defined as the sexton or beadle of a synagog. But unless you're an Episcopalian or something bizarre like that, you're not going to know what a sexton or a beadle is. So why don't I just tell you what a shamus is?

Fine. A shamus is a guy who takes care of handyman tasks around the shul, and makes sure everything is in working order—you know, like a sexton or a beadle.

A shamus is at the bottom of the pecking order of synagog functionaries, and there's a joke about that:

A rabbi, to show his humility before God, cries out in the middle of a service, "Oh, Lord, I am nobody!" The cantor, not to be bested, also cries out, "Oh, Lord, *I* am nobody!"

The shamus, deeply moved, follows suit and cries, "Oh, Lord, I am nobody!" The rabbi turns to the cantor and says, "Look who thinks he's nobody."

When pronounced SHAY-mis, shamus means a private detective, which probably comes from the fact that it's the shamus's job to guard the shul. (Sometimes also pronounced SHAH-mis in this sense.)

shanda (SHAHN-duh)

A shame, a scandal. Especially in the expression: **a shanda fur die goyim** (uh SHAHN-duh fur dee GOY-im).

To make a shanda fur die goyim is to do something embarrassing to Jews in a place where non-Jews can observe it. Understandably, this is looked on with much greater disfavor than to act like a jerk when only other Jews are around, since it makes things tougher on all of us—"those damned Jews! See what they're like?"

(Opposite: **shayner yid**. Also see **plotz**.)

Shavuos (shuh-VOO-es)

A holiday that comes in the late spring and celebrates the giving of the ten commandments to Moses.

Like most Jewish holidays (and the holidays of most religions, for that matter), Shavuos goes back to an earlier agricultural festival—the harvesting of the first fruits.

More important, Shavuos is the least famous Jewish holiday you can get off from school for. Yom Kippur and Rosh Hashonah are automatic; in New York, the public schools close down for them. Passover and Chanukah are also quite dependable. But Purim, Succos and Shavuos take some doing. As for Sh'mini Atzeres and Tisha Bov, forget it.

They're just too obscure. Even the other Jewish kids haven't heard of them.

Sometimes spelled Shavuoth. (See **Sephardim**.)

shayn, shayna (SHAYN, SHAY-nuh)
Fine; beautiful.

shayna maydala (SHAY-nuh MAY-duh-luh)
Beautiful young woman or girl.
Isn't that a beautiful way to say "beautiful young woman"? *Shayna maydala*—it's so soft and gentle.

shayner yid (SHAY-nur YID)
A dutiful Jew, a Jew of whom other Jews can be proud.
Literally, a "beautiful Jew," although the beauty being referred to here is not physical.
(Opposite: **a shanda fur die goyim**.)

shchav (properly: sh'chahv; commonly: shahv)
A soup made from sorrel or fennel or spinach.

shegetz; plural: **shkutzim** (SHAY-gits, SHKŎOTS-im)
A non-Jewish man, particularly a young man.

shekels (SHEH-kuls)
Gelt.

shema, yisroel, adonoy elohaynu, adonoy echod (shuh-MAH yis-ro-AYL ah-do-NOY el-oh-HAY-noo ah-do-NOY eh-KHAWD)
Hear, O Israel, the Lord our God, the Lord is One.
This is the most important, and most common, Jewish prayer—the last prayer you're supposed to say before dying. For thousands of years, Jews who were tortured for refusing to convert (and for other reasons, and for no reason) died with this prayer on their lips.

Shevuos (see **Shavuos**)

shicker (SHIK-ur)
Drunk.
A drunk.
Sometimes you also hear *shickered up* to mean drunk.

shicksa (SHIK-suh)
A non-Jewish woman, particularly a young woman.

shidach (SHID-ukh)
A match between a man and woman arranged by a shad-khen (qv).

shiva (SHIV-uh)
The seven days of mourning that begin after a Jewish funeral.
One speaks of "sitting shiva" because it's traditional to sit on stools or benches rather than chairs during this period. Mirrors are covered; cloth slippers are worn instead of shoes; the mourners stay home and don't work.

shkutz (shkoots)
A derogatory name for a shegetz (qv).

shlaff (shlahf)
To sleep.
Another beautiful, gentle word.
Shlaff, shlaff, mein kint—sleep, sleep, my child.

shlemiel (shluh-MEEL or -MEE-ul)
A jerk, particularly a nerdy sort of jerk.
Yiddish has more words for this concept than any other ten languages put together. Here are just a few of them: kuni lemel, nayfish, nebbish, schmuck (in the sense of dope), shlemiel, shlep, shlepper, shlump, shmageggie, shmendrik,

shmo, shnook, yutz and zhlub. There are minor variations
between these words, of course, but they all indicate in-
eptness, lack of common sense, lack of physical grace and
sex appeal, a quality of hopelessness and—how shall I put
it—well, shlumpiness.

Now—Eskimos have fourteen words for snow and one
word for anything that flies, whether it's an insect, a bird
or an airplane. We have lots of words for things that fly,
but (unless we're skiers) only one word for snow. Languages
reflect the environments in which they are spoken, the cultures of the people who speak them, and what's important
to the survival and well-being of those people.

So the question is, what was it about the environment of
the shtetl, and perhaps Jewish culture in general, that pro-
duced so many words for shlemiel? Are there actually more
Jewish shlemiels? Or are Jews just more aware of shlemiels
because it was important to be? Did Jewish shlemiels have
a higher death rate in pogroms and the like? Was it harder
for them to deal with the goyim who have surrounded and
outnumbered the Jews for 2000 years?

Don't look at me. I don't know the answers. But I sure
think they're interesting questions.

shlep

To lug; to carry something burdensome.

Also, someone who is a drag. *He's such a shlep*.

Also (a minor variation), a slob; someone who drags his
body around. **Shlepper** is another word for this meaning.

(Also see **shlemiel**.)

shlikhes (SHLIKH-us)

Prayers of penitence recited between Rosh Hashonah and
Yom Kippur.

This isn't a very important word to know, but I put it in
because I love the way it sounds.

shlimazl (shli-MAH-zul)

A born loser; someone whose luck is consistently bad.

A waiter who spills soup on a customer is a klutz. The customer he spills it on is a shlimazl.

(From the German *schlimm*—"bad" + the Hebrew *mazel*—"luck.")

shlimazl (with klutz)

shlob (see **zhlob**)

shlock (see **schlock**)

shlock-house (see **schlock-house**)

shlock-meister (see **schlockmeister**)

shlong (shlawng)

Yet another word for penis. (Also see **putz, schmuck** and **shvantz.**)

Unlike the others, shlong can't be used figuratively. It just means . . . the thing itself.

shlump (shloŏmp)
A drip; someone who drags his body around with no grace or élan whatever.
(Also see **shlemiel**.)

shm-
This sound is substituted for the beginning of a word, to convey the idea "so what's such a big deal?"
Call him a Nazi, he won't even frown,
Nazi, shmazi, says Werner von Braun. (Tom Lehrer)

sh'ma (see **shaem**—that's what I get for trying to type when I'm drunk—see **shema**)

shmageggie (shmuh-GEH-gee)
Yet another word for jerk. Shmageggie implies a kind of frantic thoughtlessness. Here's an example:
For more than thirty years I've been using Band-Aids and for more than thirty years I've been looking at the wrapper and reading a little note that says: TEAR OFF END, followed by an arrow pointing to one end of the Band-Aid, followed by PULL STRING DOWN. For all that time, I've torn open the end the arrow is pointing at, pulled on the little red string, and had it slip out in my fingers without tearing the wrapper open.
Just last week I accidentally tore open the *other* end of the wrapper, the end the arrow points away from, and when I pulled on the little red string, it ripped right through the paper like magic. Suddenly I realized: *the arrow tells you which way to pull the string*, not *which end to open!*
Now granted, Johnson & Johnson's instructions could

be clearer. But only a shmageggie could take so long to figure them out.

(Also see **shlemiel**.)

shmakhtes (SHMAKH-tus)

Isn't that a wonderful-sounding word?

(It means "tatters.")

shmaltz (see **schmaltz**)

shmata (SHMAH-tuh)

Literally, a rag.

More usually, a dress or other piece of clothing. *This shmata?! I've had it for years.*

Shmata can also be used to refer to things other than clothing: *Her! She's nothing but a shmata.*

You call it a play. I call it a shmata. This more general usage is somewhat dated.

shmeer

1. To smear, or spread, as butter on bread.
2. A bribe.
3. To bribe. (Similar in origin to the English phrase "to grease (someone's) palm."

(Also see **the whole shmeer**.)

shmeikhel (SHMEI-khul)

Literally, to smile.

More usually it means to flatter, to butter up. A **shmeikhler** is a charming con man.

shmendrik (SHMEN-drik)

Another one of the zillion Jewish words for jerk.

(Also see **shlemiel**.)

shmo

A euphemism for schmuck, shmo is much milder. Like two out of every three Jewish words, shmo means jerk.

(Also see **shlemiel**.)

shmooze (shmooz)

This is one of my favorites. It means to talk or chat in a warm, intimate way. "Shmooze" is more haymish than "chat," less invidious than "gossip," more relaxed than "talk"—no English word comes close to it. You can only shmooze with someone you feel very comfortable with—usually an old friend.

Shmooze is also a noun: *We had a good shmooze and straightened it all out.*

shmuck

Leo Rosten spells **schmuck** this way, so that no one can inadvertently mispronounce it "skmuck." I think it might be kind of amusing to hear some schmuck call someone a "skmuck" every once in a while but, personal preferences aside, the simple fact of the matter is that **schmuck** is spelled "schmuck" and I feel like a schmuck spelling **schmuck** "shmuck."

shmutz (shmŏots)

If I were king of the world, I would make shmutz the official, universal word for dirt. As it is, I have to be satisfied with merely using it in every possible situation: *just anterior to the frontal lobe, adjacent to the splendina, is some shmutz, and I wonder if perhaps that might not indicate . . .*

On entering a city totally leveled by an earthquake—nothing but rubble as far as the eye can see: *OK, the first thing we need to do is clean up some of this shmutz.*

shnaps (see **schnaps**)

shnook (shnŏŏk)

A jerk; the kind of guy who spends a night in a hotel and leaves his own towel.

(Also see **shlemiel**.)

shnorrer (SHNAWR-ur)

A beggar.

Jews have a traditional obligation to give alms to the poor, and Jewish shnorrers, being well aware of the seriousness with which most Jews treat this duty, have acquired a reputation for being brash and demanding, rather than humble and grateful. There are lots of jokes about the chutzpah of shnorrers, but since none of them are very funny, I I won't waste your time with them.

shnoz, shnozzle, shnozzola

(shnahz, SHNAHZ-ul, shnahz-OH-luh)

Kneecap.

Well, really it means nose. Everybody knows that. I was just having a little fun.

Shnoz comes from the German *Schnauze*, "snout," from which schnauzers get their name. Isn't that interesting?

I can't think of anything funny to say about shnoz, so I'm going to go on to the next definition, OK?

shofer (SHO-fur)

A guy who drives a car for a living.

That's in English. In Hebrew, a shofer is the ram's horn sounded in the synagog on Rosh Hashonah and Yom Kippur.

The shofer is several thousand years old, and was used to sound alarms in times of war, to bring down the walls of Jericho, and things like that. It has a very evocative sound and, if you shut your eyes, it's easy to imagine yourself on some desert hill 2800 years ago, looking down on the Great Temple in Jerusalem.

One of the highlights of the High Holidays, as far as I'm concerned.

shokhet, shoykhet (SHO-, SHAW- or SHOY-khet)
The person authorized to slaughter animals in the kosher manner.

Way more than just a butcher, a shokhet must know all the rules pertaining to ritual slaughter, and must be a pious and upstanding member of the community. Shokhets are certified by the rabbis of their communities. (See **glot kosher** for one example of the sort of things a shokhet has to pay attention to.)

sholent (SHAW-lent)
Traditionally, Jews aren't allowed to light a fire on shabbes. And traditionally, sholent is the solution to the problem that creates: how to have something hot to eat Saturday afternoon.

Sholent is a casserole of meat and vegetables (usually potatoes, rice and beans) that's put in the oven before sunset on Friday to roast slowly overnight and all morning (as in a crock pot). The result of all the juices mixing together is spectacular.

The German poet Heinrich Heine thought that the Christian Church, "which borrowed so much that was good from ancient Judaism," made a big mistake in not adopting sholent as well. A convert himself, he figured that reason would lead Jews to Christianity, and that sholent "alone holds them together in their old faith."

sholom (see **shalom**)

sholom aleichem (see **shalom aleichem**)

shpilkes (SHPIL-kus)
Literally, "pins." But to say someone has shpilkes means

they can't sit still, that they have ants in their pants. (It's short for *shpilkes in tokhis*—"pins in your ass.")

I once went on a long trip to Baja California with a group of people, one of whom had the most goyisha name conceivable: Gay Bishop. (Even a gay bishop is less goyish than someone *named* Gay Bishop.)

To go along with her name, Gay had a punim (face) so goyish that it looked like no Jew had ever lived in the same county as one of her ancestors. In spite of all this, she had picked up quite a bit of Yiddish, the result of a checkered past littered with broken-hearted Jewish princes. Gay was proud of her command of Yiddish, but she kept quiet about it.

So while Tak Tsuchiya, who was in a Jewish fraternity in college, asked me if I was a "member of the tribe," and while Tom Hayes and Nancy Shine (not Jewish, despite her name) tossed around "shlep" and "schmuck" and other well-known Jewish words, Gay sat quietly and bided her time.

Then one day, when I was uncomfortably fidgeting in my seat, she struck. "What's the matter," she said, "you got shpilkes or something?" I think the expression on my face must have been worth the wait.

shpritz (shprits)

To spray, including to spray with spit, as when talking excitedly.

Shpritz is used as a noun too. *Give me a shpritz of that whipped cream.*

Shpritz also has a figurative sense—to put down, needle, tease. *So, Shelly, he doesn't know any better, he starts shpritzing these guys* (Lenny Bruce).

shpritzer (SHPRITS-er)

A sprayer of any kind. Those seltzer-making bottles the Three Stooges were always squirting in people's faces are called shpritzers.

shtarker (SHTAHRK-kur)

A tough guy.

"Ah," he said wearily, "another New York shtarker" (Pete Hamill, *The Dirty Piece*).

My concept of a shtarker is a guy who wears a wool suit without underwear (Lenny Bruce).

(From the German *stark*, "strong.")

shtetl (SHTEHT- or SHTAYT-ul)

The kind of small rural settlement eastern European Jews typically lived in, because they weren't allowed to live in the cities.

The shtetl is the world of *Fiddler on the Roof*. The isolation and lack of knowledge of the outside world that characterized life in the shtetl is difficult for us to imagine. Jerzy Kosinski's *The Painted Bird* is an almost unbearably powerful evocation of life in similar, non-Jewish, Polish villages. It's an incredible book, if you can stand it.

shtick; plural: **shticklach** (SHTIK-lahkh)

Oy.

Well, originally, literally, a piece of something. *A shtick dreck* is a piece of shit. (Shtick never takes "of" after it.)

From there it came to mean a piece (a part) of a show-business routine: *My Las Vegas lounge shtick is going over great. I'm another Frank Dell.*

From there it came to mean a *kind* of shtick: *I just can't get into that slapstick shtick* (say that three times quickly). Or: *I think the character would be more believable without all those shmaltzy shticklach.*

From there it came to mean a con: *You fell for a shtick like that?*

And from there it came to mean a part of one's neurotic way of relating to other people: *Oh, he's into his "nobody loves me" shtick again.*

shtunk (shtoͦonk)

A rat. A louse. A stinker.

shtup (shtoͦop)

To fuck. (Literally, to push.)

Also see **no khoupie, no shtupie**.

shtuss (shtoͦos)

A commotion.

Also, nonsense, along the line of "sound and fury, sig-nifying nothing."

What's all this shtuss about?

shul (shoͦol)

A synagog, a Jewish temple.

It tells you a lot about Jewish culture that the word for house of worship means "school." The Hebrew name, *bes midrash*, means the same thing—house of study.

In the shtetl, the shul was like a community center or clubhouse. Many men spent more time studying (and shmoozing) in shul than they did working. Some shuls were open day and night. In America, however, most Jews relate to shuls in much the same way as Christians relate to churches.

Here's a joke about shuls:

Every weekend, Harry and Mort meet at the track. And every weekend, Harry wins and Mort loses. Finally Mort says, "Harry, tell me—what's the secret of your success?"

"It's simple. Every Saturday morning before I come out here, I go to shul and pray."

So next Saturday morning, Mort goes to shul and prays for success at the track. And that afternoon, he loses every race.

"I don't understand it," he says. "I prayed all morning."

"What shul did you go to?" Harry asks.

"Anshe Mizpah."

"Well, no wonder. That's for trotters."

shvantz (shvahnts)

Yet another word for penis.

(Also see **putz, schmuck** and **shlong**.)

Shvantz can also be used figuratively, to mean a person who's a prick.

shvartza (SHVAHRTS-uh)

A black, a Negro.

Since many Jewish households had black "cleaning ladies" who came in once or twice a week, "the shvartza" came to mean "the maid."

While I'm on the subject, I'd like to take the opportunity to say something nice about the woman who was our cleaning lady for many years—Lucy Butler. I don't know exactly *what* to say about her except that she was some sort of saint, always managing to be loving and helpful under conditions that drove at least one weaker person batty (of course I was was exposed to them more frequently).

Shvartza isn't in itself a term of contempt; it has a more or less neutral value. But it can be (and often is) used contemptuously: *he dresses like a shvartza* (by me, this is a compliment).

shver (shvayr)

Hard; difficult.

(Also see **'siz shver tsu zein a yid**.)

shviger (SHVIG-ur)

Mother-in-law.

shvitz, shvitzer (shvits, SHVITS-ur)

To sweat.

A shvitzer is someone who sweats a lot and, by extension, it has also come to mean a nervous suitor.

It can also mean braggart, although it's not clear to me why braggarts would be famous for sweating.

shvoogie (SHVŎOG-ee)

A somewhat more derogatory term for a black than "shvartza."

Shvoogie usually implies disrespect or even contempt, but is still much milder than a word like "nigger." It's mostly used in a light, humorous vein. *Beat Dunbar?! Are you kidding? They're all seven-foot shvoogies!*

simcha (SIM-khuh)

A joyous event; a celebration.

the six million

Ask almost anybody how many people the Nazis murdered outside of combat and they'll tell you six million. But that's not even close. The number is actually *twelve* million (ten million civilians and two million prisoners of war), of whom six million—aha!—were Jews.

Now I know we're smarter and more sensitive and just all around better than everybody else, but it does seem to me that just because the six million Russians, Poles, Serbs, Gypsies, homosexuals, communists, socialists, anarchists, pacifists and, by the way, Christians (because anyone who was a *real* Christian in Nazi Germany and didn't get out ended up in a concentration camp)—just because these people weren't Jewish doesn't mean they don't count.

I don't think it's so hard to understand how survivors of the Holocaust can raise money to help Israel do to the Palestinians what Germany did to the Jews when you realize that these same people always refer to the six million victims of the Nazis as if the six million non-Jews didn't exist.

But they did exist and just like the Jews, they had organs, dimensions, senses, affections, passions. If you pricked them, they bled. If you poisoned them, they died. So I think we owe it to them to remember their deaths too.

'siz shver tsu zein a yid (siz SHVAYR tsoo zein uh YID)
It's hard to be a Jew.

With 613 separate commandments to follow, hundreds of brawkhas to say every day, all kinds of delicious food you can't eat and neighborhood louts beating the crap out of you every day, it's easy to see where this saying came from. Here in America though, we have it easy.

So far.

sports (see **shvartza**)

strudel (SHTROO-dul)
A Hungarian pastry generally acknowledged to be the most delicious thing you can eat. (I'm talking here about real homemade strudel, of course.) It's made of a very thin dough rolled around a filling of fruit, chopped nuts, butter and sugar. It could be better, but how?

stuffed cabbage
Cabbage leaves rolled into tubes, stuffed with chopped meat and rice, and cooked in tomato sauce.

Succos (SŎOK-is)
A seven-day holiday that comes in the fall, five days after Yom Kippur. The present-day Succos shadows a much older harvest festival.

Succos gets its name from *sukas* (SŎOK-uhz)—small huts that all Jews, rich and poor, are commanded to set up and live in during the holiday, in remembrance of the forty years the Hebrews spent in similar structures while wandering in the wilderness. Hardly anybody bothers to build sukas anymore, much less live in them.

Sukas are supposed to be set up outdoors, so you can see the stars through the roof of vines and boughs. But the only sukas I've seen have been in temple basements. Through their roofs you could see the beige sound paneling on the ceiling.

Sometimes spelled Succoth. (See **Sephardim**.)

'svet gornisht helfen (svet GAWR-nisht HELF-un)
It won't help a bit.

synagog (SIN-uh-gahg)
Greek for "shul."

Reform congregations call their shuls temples rather than synagogs.

T

taka (TAH-kuh)

What a...!

For example, *taka metsiah!*—what a bargain (sarcastically, that is).

tallis (TAHL-is)

A fringed shawl traditionally worn by Jews when praying. Typically white with thick blue or black stripes across it, the tallis is one of the nicer ritual touches in the Jewish religion.

Talmud (TAHL-mood)

The massive (sixty-three-book) compilation of commentaries on the Torah, commentaries on the commentaries, commentaries on the commentaries on the commentaries, etc. In the Talmud are found most of the customs and rules by which Jews have traditionally lived.

The Talmud is divided into six main sections which cover agriculture, festivals and holidays, sex and marriage, civil and criminal laws, sacred rituals, personal hygiene and which foods are kosher to eat.

About half the books of the Talmud are composed of two parts: the older Mishnah, written in Hebrew, and the newer Gemora, written in Aramaic. (Newer is a relative term here, since the most recent parts of the Gemora were written 1500 years ago.) The other books only have Mishnah.

Actually, two Talmuds were compiled, one in Jerusalem and another in Babylonia about a century later. Some of the Jerusalem Talmud has been lost and, in any case, the Babylonian Talmud is considered to be more authoritative.

Over the centuries following the writing of the Gemora, some additional commentaries were added by Talmud scholars. These are called **toseftot.** (In Israel, you can order a steak or hamburger with "toseftot." You get french fries, vegetables, etc.—in other words, "the extras.")

The role of the Talmud in forming Jewish character is obvious. Take, for example, the section which treats the duties of Jewish boys in high school:

Thou shalt not take shop courses of any sort, nor shalt thou wear cowboy boots or drive a pickup truck. Neither shalt thou rebuild a carburetor, nor hang little dice made out of foam from thy rearview mirror. For these are the things which the goyim do.

Studying the Talmud developed to a very high degree the ability to make fine distinctions, to understand abstract concepts, and to manipulate verbal constructs. The reason there are so many Jewish writers, scientists, teachers and lawyers today is that there were so many Jewish talmudists 500 (and 1500) years ago.

(Talmud means "study" in Hebrew.)

Talmud Torah (TAHL-mood TOH-ruh)
1. A school where one studies Talmud and Torah (qv).
2. In the United States, a Hebrew school.

tanta (TAHN-tuh)
Aunt.

tata, tatela, tatenyu (TAH-tuh, -tuh-luh, -ten-yoo)
Father.

Tatala, the diminutive, is often used to address little boys, probably originally as a way to fool the evil eye— "don't be tempted into taking a life this young; this is really an old man." (As you can see, the evil eye is *really* stupid.) See **mieskeit** for another example of this approach.

Tatenyu means either "dear father" or "dear God." *Oy, tatenyu, what have I done to deserve this!*

tefillin (tuh-FIL-un)
Phylacteries.
That's what they always say. So, naturally, you have to go look up phylacteries (unless, of course, you just assume they're those things they sell in drug stores for the prevention of disease—in which case you get funny stares from pharmacists when you say, "Lemme have a package of those— whadayacallum?—*tefillin*. You got any with ribs?").

Phylacteries, it turns out, are two small leather boxes attached to long leather straps. Orthodox Jews wear one on their left arm and another high on their forehead while praying, in obedience to the Biblical command: "and it shall be for a sign unto thee upon thine hand, and for a memorial between thine eyes, that the Lord's law may be in thy mouth" (Exodus 13:9).

Inside the phylacteries are tiny pieces of parchment on which are written passages from the Bible (like in a mezuzah). In other words, phylacteries are . . . tefillin, and that's the only things phylacteries are. In that case, since we already have the word "tefillin," what is the purpose of the word "phylacteries"?

I'm glad you asked me that. The purpose of the word phylacteries is to make something Jewish sound goyish and official.

"Tefillin? What is that, some Jewish thing?"

"Phylacteries? Hmmm, sounds important."

You can see the goyim keeping a word like "tefillin" out of their dictionaries. But "phylacteries"?—no way.

temple
What Reform Jews call shul.

T.L. (see **tokhis lecker**)

tokhis, tochis (TAW or TŎO-khis)
An ass—I don't mean like Balaam's ass—well, he had *two* asses—or maybe more, I don't know—but I mean, not a donkey, but rather, you know, your—your rear end—no, not the one with the universal joint and the leaf springs—oh, you know, your tokhis.

tokhis lekher (TAW-khus LEKH-ur)
An ass-kisser. (Literally, an "ass licker.")

T.O.T.
Short for **tokhis afn tish** (TAW-khis AH-fun TISH)—

"ass on the table." Equivalent to the English "lay your cards on the table" or "put your ass on the line." *All right, let's talk straight business—T.O.T."*

toushie, toush (TŎŌSH-ee)
A child's word for tokhis. Also used by adults. More or less equivalent to "bottom," "behind" or "rear end."

Torah (TOH-ruh)
Strictly, the scroll on which the five books of Moses are written. The Torah is kept in the ark in shul. You read from it using a silver pointer with a little hand at the end.
More usually, the text of the five books of Moses.
Sometimes Torah means, more generally, the entire range of Jewish knowledge.
(Also see **khoumish**.)

trayf
Not kosher.
(Literally, trayf means torn from the flesh of a living animal, the way a dog might do it. Imagine a society where you had to tell people to kill animals before eating them and you get some idea of how old Judaism is.)

trombenik (TRAHM-ben-ik)
A braggart; an egotistical bore.
(From a Polish word meaning "brass horn.")

trosk (see **frosk**)

tsadik (TSAH-dik)
A man distinguished for his piety and/or scholarship.

tsatska, tsatskie (see **chachka, chachkie**)

tsimis (TSIM-us)

1. A stew of carrots, prunes, raisins, noodles and other fruits and vegetables.

2. A fuss; a big deal; an involved, complicated mess. Often in the expression *a big tsimis* or *a whole tsimis*.

tsitsis

The Bible commands Jews to wear "fringes on the borders of their garments . . . that ye may look upon [them] and remember all the commandments of the Lord, and do them; and . . . seek not after your own heart . . . which ye use to go a whoring" (Numbers 15:38–39).

Strong stuff, eh? Just offhand it sounds like it might be more fun *not* to wear the fringes. But many Orthodox Jews don't agree, and the fringes they wear are called tsitsis.

Tsitsis are worn on the tallis, and on a strange undershirt called an *arba kanfis* or a *tallis kotun*. (It's strange, yes, but not as amazing as the Mormons' "temple underwear," which will withstand the full force of a nuclear blast at point-blank range.)

Since the commandment says that tsitsis must be seen, Orthodox men let them hang out from underneath their vests or jackets. This looks very bizarre. I'm not sure what effect it has on "going a whoring," but it certainly must cut down on getting it for free.

tsu gezunt (tsoo guh-ZŎONT)

God bless you; a response to a sneeze.

(Literally, "to health.")

tsu gut iz umgezunt (TSOO gŏot iz ŎOM-guh-ZŎONT)

Too good is unhealthy (said of a child who's too well behaved).

tsuris (TSŎOR-, TSOOR- or TSAWR-us)

As words for trouble go, "trouble" is one of the better ones. But it simply isn't in the same league with "tsuris." It's hard even to say "tsuris" without feeling vaguely worried and depressed.

tukhis (see **tokhis**)

tummel (TŎOM-ul)

A commotion; a lot of noise and excitement.

tummler (TŎOM-ler)

Someone who makes a commotion. Particularly someone who's always making jokes—a life of the party.

Also, someone hired to do that professionally at a resort in the borsht belt (qv), to keep the guests entertained. Moss Hart once worked as a tummler, as did many famous comics.

two Jews, three synagogs

This sums up the Jewish love for cantankerous intellectual disputes. Today one of the synagogs would be a union hall, another would be a political club, and the third would be a growth experience.

The only thing two Jews can agree on is how much a third Jew should give to charity.

U

unaweza kuniambia kiasi gani nauli ya kwenda Minsk?
Can you tell me how much the one-way fare to Minsk is?

You may not get much of a chance to use this phrase, since it's in Swahili and there are no direct connections between East Africa and Byelorussia at the present time. I just put it in because I'm getting pretty sick of nothing but Jewish expressions, Jewish expressions, Jewish expressions

Unaweza kuniambia kiasi gani nauli ya kwenda Minsk?

till they're coming out of my ears! I mean, after a certain point, it begins to get on your nerves.

You have it easy. You look up a couple of words and put the book away and space out in front of the tube, but I have to keep cranking out these definitions. I need a change of pace, a vacation. I see giraffes loping across the veldt. From out by the baobab tree, I hear the hahdeedah birds calling me . . . hah dee dah . . . hah dee dah . . . had dee dah . . .

Oh, well, enough of this. Back to the old grind. What's next—ungepachkit? OK, let's do it.

ungepachkit (OON-guh-PAHCH-ket)

Doesn't that have a great Jewish sound? I mean, there's a word that couldn't in a billion years pass for French or Italian. When you say "ungepachkit," you *know* you're talking Yiddish.

But do you know what you're saying? Granted the word has a great sound, like someone's yiddisha grandfather slurping borsht through his beard, but what does it mean?

You don't know, do you? Hey, don't apologize. What the hell—if you already *knew* every Jewish expression, what would you need this book for? Right?

Uh . . . ungepachkit. Ungepachkit means tastelessly, ornately overdone, thrown together with no sense of consistency or restraint, like those buildings Howard Roark blew up in *The Fountainhead* or, for that matter, almost any hotel in Miami Beach.

Ungepachkit doesn't refer to just architecture. For example, the start of this definition is ungepachkit.

Here's the classic joke about ungepachkit:

In his well-to-do middle years, Sidney has become a connoisseur of modern art, and he wants to get his old friend Myron enthusiastic about it too. So one day he takes Myron to the Museum of Modern Art.

The first painting they come to is a white canvas ten feet

157

square with one vertical black line straight down the middle of it. "Can you sense the savage sparseness of this piece?" Sidney kvells. "There's so much the artist is saying by what he leaves unsaid."

Anxious to learn, Myron nods uncertainly.

The next painting is another huge white square, but this time the black line is slightly off vertical. "Can you feel the incredible tension this is generating?" says Sidney. "Nothing but that one dramatic line, *almost* but *not quite* vertical. What raw power!"

Myron says "hmmm," like he's beginning to understand.

The third painting they come to is a slightly smaller white square on which two black lines cross each other at an angle. "It's your turn now," Sidney says. "What do you think of this one?"

Myron studies the painting intently for a few moments and says, "Well, if you ask me, Sidney, it's a little ungepachkit."

V

varnishkas (see **kasha varnishkas**)

vay iz mier (VAY iz meer, or VAY iz MEER)
  Woe is me.
  (Also see **oy vay**.)

vershtay? (see **fershtay**? Fershtay?)

ven es zol helfen gott betten, volt men shoyn tsugedungen menschen (ven es zawl HELF-un GOTT BET-tun, vawlt men shoyn TSOO-geh-DŎONG-un MENSH-un)
  If it did any good to pray, they'd be hiring people to do it.

ven ikh zol handlen mit licht, volt die zun nisht untergegangen (ven ikh zawl HAHND-lun mit LIKHT, vawlt die ZOON nisht ŎON-ter-geh-GAHNG-un)
  If I sold candles, the sun would never set.

veren zol fun dir a blintsa, un fun im a katz, er zol dikh oysfressen, un mit dir zikh dervargen, volt men fun eikh bayda poter gevoren (VAYR-un zawl fun DEER ah BLINTS-uh, awn fun EEM ah KAHTZ, ayr zawl dikh OYS-fres-un, awn mit deer zeekh dayr-VAHRG-un, vawlt men fun EIKH BAY-da PAW-ter guh-VAW-run)
  May you turn into a blintz, and he into a cat, and may

159

he eat you up and choke on you, so we can get rid of both of you.

ver vayst? (vayr vayst)
Who knows?

vie gott in Odess (vee GAWT in oh-DES)
(To live) "like God in Odessa."
This was the greatest image of luxury the Jews of the shtetl could conjure up. Today, of course, we would say, "like Bob Dylan in Malibu."

vie gott in Odess

vie narish menschen zeinen—bagroben zay aynem, vaynen zay; bagruben zay tsvay, tantsen zay (vee NAHRish MENSH-un ZEIN-un—bah-GRO-bun zay AYN-um, VAY-nun zay; bah-GRO-bun zay TSVAY, TANTS-un zay)
(A comment on weddings:) How foolish people are— bury one person and they cry; bury two and they dance.

vie a yoven in suka (vee ah YO-vun in SŎOK-uh)
Like a bull in a china shop. (Literally, "like a pagan in a Succos hut.")
(Also see **Succos** and **alle yevonim hoben ayn ponim**.)

vos (vaws or vus)

What.

vos der mensch ken alts ibertrachten, ken der ergster soyna im nisht vinchen (vaws dayr MENSH ken ahlts IB-ur-trahkh-tun, ken dayr AYRG-stur SOYN-uh eem nisht VINCH-un)

What people can think up for themselves, their own worst enemies couldn't wish upon them.

vu shtet es geshreiben? (voo SHTAYT es guh-SHREIB-un)

Where is it written? (Where in the Talmud or Torah or other holy scripture does it say that I can't do this, or that I have to do that?)

W

wape salamu zangu vifuniko vya visugu vya miguu zako
Give my regards to your corn pads.
OK, I promise, no more Swahili. I just couldn't resist that one.

the whole megillah (muh-GIL-uh)
The whole (long, detailed, boring) story.
(Also see **Megillah** and **Purim**.)

the whole shmeer
The whole thing, whatever it is.
And how much for the whole shmeer?

the whole shmeeyegee (shmee-YEHG-ee)
Also means the whole thing. (Don't confuse this with **shmageggie**.)
(Probably a diminutive version of **the whole shmeer**.)

Y

yamulka (YAH- or, much less frequently, YAHR-moōl-kuh)

A small, round cap, covering just the top of the head, worn in shul and, by more religious Jews, at all times.

Similar skullcaps are also worn by Catholic and Anglican priests, including the Pope, and by many Muslims. I was once in the remote mountain town of Pec (say "pesh"), Yugoslavia, and all the men wandering along the rutted dirt street wore yamulkas.

There's nothing in the Bible that commands Jews to cover their heads, so there's some question how the practice got started. Most scholars support the following theory:

Around 550 B.C. several Jewish boys at Babylon State (the Nippur campus) were pledged to Gimel Omega Yod. They were so proud of having gotten into this previously restricted fraternity (which wouldn't even take Hittites!) that they continued to wear their pledge beanies all their adult lives. The custom spread because of a practical advantage— yamulkas keep your bald spot warm.

Yamulka is often spelled yarmulka; in fact, it usually is. But you rarely hear anyone pronounce the **r**. I don't want to make any allegations I can't back up, but it seems that this might well be yet another tentacle of the pervasive Sephardic **th** plot. See **Sephardim** for the frightening details.

yenta (YEN-tuh)

A pesty, petty, gossipy housewife.

There's a button that reads: Marcel Proust is a yenta. It's his obsession with small details that earns him the title.

Here's the classic yenta joke:

A yenta is riding on a bus. She turns to the man next to her and says, "Excuse me, mister, I hope you don't mind my asking, but are you Jewish?"

"Well, I don't mind your asking but, no, actually, I'm not." He nods pleasantly and goes back to reading his paper.

A couple of minutes later the yenta pipes up again. "Excuse me, mister, but are you *sure* you're not Jewish?"

"Yes, madam, I'm quite sure." He refolds his paper emphatically, and goes back to reading.

A few minutes later, the yenta says, "Listen, mister, I'm sorry to bother you again, but are you *absolutely sure* you're not Jewish?"

The man has had it. "OK, lady, you win. I'm Jewish. All right? Whatever you say. I'm Jewish."

"You know, it's funny," says the yenta. "You don't look it."

And—lucky you—here's another one (for some reason, many yenta jokes are about non-Jewish men being bothered on some kind of public transportation):

Professor McCallister is riding the Broadway Limited, on his way to Chicago to deliver a lecture. As he's drifting off to sleep, he hears a woman's voice from the Pullman berth just below him saying, "Oy, am I toisty!"

He turns over and begins drifting off again, when a second time the voice says, "Oy! Am I toisty!"

Now I know what you're expecting. You think she's going to say it a third time, and then he's going to do something. Most jokes go by threes like that. But Professor McCallister is very nervous about his speech the next day, and he's a very high-strung kind of guy anyway. He doesn't care if the joke is funny or not; he just wants to get some sleep.

So instead of waiting for her to say it a third time, like he should, he gets up after the second time, walks to the end of the car, fills a little paper cup with water, brings it back, and hands it to the woman through the curtain of her Pullman berth.

"Here, madam," he says, "perhaps this will slake your thirst and then we can both slip blissfully into the arms of Morpheus." (He's one of those old-fashioned, gentlemanly professors.)

The yenta in the lower berth thanks him and drinks up the water.

Professor McCallister climbs back into his berth and is just drifting off to his well-deserved rest when the yenta begins to sigh: "Oy, vas I toisty!"

yeshiva (yuh-SHEE-vuh)

Today, a Jewish seminary; a place where rabbis are trained.

Formerly, any advanced school of Jewish studies.

In the United States, yeshiva is also used to refer to Jewish high schools and even grammar schools.

yeshiva bokher (yuh-SHEE-vuh BAW-kher)

A student at a yeshiva. (Literally, "yeshiva boy"—beformerly only boys were allowed to study at a yeshiva.)

Therefore, an unworldly type. Someone with his head in the clouds (and his nose in a book).

Yid

A Jew.

(From the German *Juede*, from the Hebrew *Yehuda*, Judah—the name of an ancient Jewish country, from the name of one of Jacob's sons.)

Yiddish (YID-ish)

The language of the Jews of eastern Europe, a blend of Hebrew, Slavic and (about 70 percent) German.

With a small **y**, "yiddish" (and "yiddisha") are the Yiddish words for "Jewish."

Yiddish is written in Hebrew characters and, like Hebrew, from right to left. So what you'd think would be the back of a Yiddish book is actually the front, and vice versa.

Moishe Ginsburg, star investigative reporter for a Yiddish newspaper, comes running up to the editor's desk with his notebook in his hand.

"Chief!" he shouts, "I've got a story that will tear this town wide open. Hold the back page!"

yiddisha kup (YID-ish-uh KUP)

Jewish brains. (Literally, Jewish head.)

There are many stories about the resourceful cleverness of Jews, usually in the kind of adverse situations that made such cleverness necessary. For example, there's the one about Rabbi Ezra. The Inquisition has come to his small town in Spain, and the inquisitor who has brought it is a famous anti-Semite.

The inquisitor assembles all the Jews in the town square and says to Rabbi Ezra, "I have put two slips of paper in this hat. On one I've written the word "life"; if you pick it, your people will live. On the other slip, I've written the word "death"; if you pick that slip, your people will perish. If your God is so great, let him guide your hand."

Rabbi Ezra realizes that the word "death" is written on both slips. So he reaches into the hat, picks out a slip and, without looking at it, puts it in his mouth and swallows it.

"What are you doing?" shouts the inquisitor. "How will we know what the slip says?"

"That's no problem," says Rabbi Ezra. "Look at the slip in the hat. If it reads 'life,' then obviously the slip I swallowed read 'death.' But if it reads 'death,' then obviously the slip I swallowed read 'life.'"

(Also see **goyisha kup**.)

yiddisha mama (YID-ish-uh MAH-muh)
Jewish mother. (See **mother (Jewish)**.)

yiddisha mazel (YID-ish-uh MAH-zul)
Jewish luck.
The kind of luck about which the song says, "if it wasn't for bad luck, I wouldn't have no luck at all."
(Also see **goyisha mazel**.)

yikhes (YIKH-us)
Prestige; status.
Mr. Weisberg comes to Cleveland to see Mr. Berman, the president of a synagog he'd like to sell some supplies to. Since he has an hour to kill before his appointment, he decides to have lunch at the kosher restaurant down the

block from the shul. He strikes up a conversation with the man he's sharing his table with and happens to mention Berman's name.

"That momzer!" says the man. "May he grow like an onion, with his head in the ground!"

"Who? Berman?!" says another customer who's overheard the conversation. "I curse the day he first drew breath!"

"Yes," chimes in the owner, from behind the cash register. "I'd call him a putz, but it would be unfair to all the other putzes."

Needless to say, Weisberg is shaken up by all this. When he goes to see Berman, he can't help but ask him how he likes being president of the shul.

"Well, to be honest with you, it's an enormous amount of work. And a lot of aggravation too."

"Then why do you do it?" Weisberg asks.

"Oh, I don't know," Berman says. "For the yikhes, I suppose."

Yinglish (YING-lish)

Yiddish and English combined, as in the word *boychik*.

yisgadal v'yiskadash (yis-guh-DAHL vuh-yis-kuh-DAHSH)

The opening words of the Kaddish (qv). They mean, "May God be great! May God be sanctified!"

yiskor (YIS-kur)

A memorial service for the dead, held four times a year during Passover, Shavuos, Succos and Yom Kippur.

Yom Kippur (yum KIP-ur or YAWM ki-POOR)

The holiest of Jewish holidays, occurring ten days after Rosh Hashonah in the early fall. With Rosh Hashonah, one of the two high holidays.

Yom Kippur means "the day of atonement," and is also called by that name. It's a fast day on which the sins of the past year are repented and absolution for them is asked. You're supposed to rededicate your life by asking other people for forgiveness, making peace with God and setting New Year's resolutions for yourself.

(Also see **kol nidre** and **shofer**.)

yontif, yuntif (YAWN-tif)

A holiday.

People typically say "it's yontif" rather than "it's a yontif."

(From the Hebrew *yom tov*, "good day.")

yortsite (YAWR- or YAHR-tsait)

The anniversary of someone's death.

A **yortsite candle**, designed to burn the whole day— from sunset to sunset—is lit.

(Literally, "a year's time.")

yutz

A jerk.

(Also see **shlemiel**.)

Z

zaftig (ZAHF-tik)

A wonderful word for a wonderful concept. Literally meaning "juicy," zaftig describes a woman who is buxom, juicily plump—although it's sometimes used merely as a euphemism for "fat."

zayda (ZAY-duh)

Grandfather.

zaftig

zei gezunt (ZEI guh-ZŎONT)
 Be healthy.
 (Also see **gay gezunt**.)

zhlub (zhluhb or zhlawb, **not** shlub)
 A shlumpy jerk.
 (Also see **shlemiel**.)

zies, zieskeit (zees, ZEES-keit)
 Sweet, sweetness.
 A small child is often referred to as a zieskeit (or, if you're worried about the evil eye, as a mieskeit).
 Oh, my darling little zieskeit, come give your bouba a kiss.

Zionism (ZEI-un-iz-um)
 A political belief widely (but not universally) held by Jews (and some others) that the Jewish people have a special right to the land of Palestine.
 It's possible to admire many things about Israel, to be proud of its accomplishments, to be glad it's there as a place of refuge, and to still be disgusted by the Israeli government's treatment of the Palestinian people, or by its close ties with South Africa. In fact, many Israelis feel just that way.
 The important point here is that a Jew is not automatically or necessarily a supporter of Israel (although the vast majority of present-day American Jews certainly are).

zolst vaksen tsibulas in dayn pupik! (zawlst VAHK-sun TSIB-uh-luhs in dayn PŎOP-ik)
 May onions grow in your navel! (In other words, may you be buried in the ground, where this could happen.)

Zolst vaksen tsibulas in dayn pupik!

zolst vaksen vie a tsibula, mitn kup in drayrd (zawlst VAHK-sun vee ah TSIB-uh-luh, mitn KUP in DRAYRD)

May you grow like an onion, with your head in the ground!

zug nisht (ZŌOG or ZAWG nisht)

Don't say anything (about whatever we've just been talking about). *Here he comes. Zug nisht.*

Also, "don't talk about it. I don't want to hear about it."

ON THE RIGHT WAY
TO BE JEWISH

What are you talking about, "the right way to be Jewish"? There is no "right way" to be Jewish.

Exactly. But not everybody sees it that way. Some people feel that a Jew who doesn't have a deep reverence for the Jewish heritage, the Yiddish language and the Jewish religion isn't really a "good" Jew.

My idea of a "good Jew" is quite different from this, although just as deeply rooted in the Jewish tradition. It's identical to my idea of a good person: a mensch, someone with rakhmones.

Now it seems to me that no one with rakhmones can support Israel's present policies toward the Palestinian people, which are about the same as this country's policies toward the American Indians in the nineteenth century. And it seems to me that no mensch can accept traditional practices and beliefs without questioning their actual effect on people.

I mention all this to counter criticisms from "the-more-Jewish-the-better" school concerning various comments in this book. These are the kind of people who are always making lists of famous Jews. This is such a common way of thinking that when Carl Reiner asks that archetypical Jew, the 2013-Year-Old Man (Mel Brooks), who he thinks is the greatest person that ever lived, Brooks asks: "Jewish?...or anybody?"

An interesting thing about famous Jews is that the real biggies were almost all nonreligious or antireligious. Einstein disliked organized religion, was never a practicing Jew and, despite his oft-quoted, more-or-less deist beliefs, was for all intents and purposes a secular socialist. Marx was of course an atheist. Freud was antireligious. Spinoza was excommunicated. Woody Allen never goes to shul. And Jesus, of course, was not exactly a favorite of the Jewish establishment of his time.

Anyway, I have no apologies to make for writing a dictionary of Jewish expressions that doesn't seep with nostalgia for life in the shtetl, present the Jewish religion as the greatest collection of human truths yet assembled, or claim that the state of Israel can do no wrong. There are lots of ways to be Jewish, and every one of them is OK.

(I just hope this keeps the JDL death squad from my door.)

APPENDIX B

WHERE TO FIND
GOOD JEWISH FOOD

I feel a little funny telling you about all these wonderful Jewish dishes, because if you live in Oklahoma City or someplace, the only way you're going to find out what they taste like is to buy them canned or bottled or frozen (if you can even do that), and canned or bottled or frozen just isn't the same.

Even if you live in a major city, it can be really hard to find good Jewish food. For example, I live in the San Francisco Bay area (which is the fifth largest metropolitan area in the country), and I don't know of a single really good Jewish restaurant here.

I went into one the other day with a friend of mine who's a bit of a hypochondriac. I ordered a glass of tea and he said, "I'll have some too... and make sure the glass is clean."

A little while later, the waiter came back with our two teas. "OK," he said, "which one of you wanted the clean glass?"

Fortunately, things aren't quite so grim everywhere. The word from L.A. is Art's Deli on Ventura in Studio City; Langer's at Seventh and Alvarado; the Haimish Bakery on Pico near Doheny; and Nate and Al's in Beverly Hills. For atmosphere, and a wide selection of good restaurants

(Canter's being the most famous), wander down Fairfax from Melrose to just south of Pico. Buy a raisin pumpernickel and participate in the great Fairfax Avenue raisin war. (By the time you read this, there'll be no bread left— just a loaf of solid raisins.)

My spies in Chicago seem to agree on Sam and Hy's in Skokie. There was also some talk of The Bagel at Devon and Kedzie and The Belden at Belden and Clark.

In Philadelphia, the Marion Deli in Marion is recommended, and Hymie's in Bala Cynwyd is described as "sensational." Janice Byer says Rubin's is the best Jewish restaurant in Boston. And everybody mentions Wolfie's in Miami Beach.

But, as is true for so many different cuisines, if you want the best, New York is where you'll get it—and usually for less money (I'm just talking about restaurants).

The very best Jewish food I've ever had has been at the B&H Dairy Lunch on Second Avenue between Seventh and St. Marks, and at Yonah Schimmel's Knishery on Houston near Forsyth.

While you're down on the Lower East Side, you'll want to hit Russ and Daughters appetizing store, Ben's Cheese Shop and Moishe's Bakery (all on Houston between Allen and Orchard).

For pickles (I mean, for *pickles!*), go to the corner of Hester and Essex. Guss' Pickles is down Hester on your left, the Pickleman is up Essex on your left, and just beyond it is L. Hollander Pickles. (This is not the easiest section of the book to write, sitting here in Oakland at four in the morning, drooling on my keyboard.)

OK—Gertel's Kosher Bakery is on Hester across from Guss'. For bialys, you want Kossar's on Grand between Essex and Norfolk. For candy, Economy Candy on Essex at Rivington. For the best Roumanian pastrami, Bernstein's-on-Essex between Orchard and Rivington. And for dairy, there's Ratner's on Delancey between Norfolk and Suffolk, the Grand Dairy at Grand and Ludlow, and the Garden Cafeteria at East Broadway and Rutgers.

Let me pause for a minute here to recommend a book. Zelda Stern's *The Complete Guide to Ethnic New York* (St. Martins, 1980—$7) not only does a terrific job of covering Jewish food but is equally impressive with sixteen other cuisines—everything from Czech to West Indian. And she includes sightseeing and gift shops as well.

Ms. Stern talks about several restaurants I haven't tried, but based on her taste in restaurants I have tried, I trust her judgment. So I'll pass some of her recommendations on to you: Sammy's Roumanian Jewish on Chrystie near Delancey; Fine and Schapiro's on 72nd between Broadway and Amsterdam; and the Second Avenue Kosher Deli on (you guessed it) Second Avenue, at Tenth Street.

On the Upper West Side, there are three great food stores: Barney Greengrass on Amsterdam between 86th and 87th; Murray's Sturgeon on Broadway between 89th and 90th (these two specialize in fish); and Zabar's on Broadway near 80th (which specializes in everything under the sun).

Alan Levinson says the Carnegie Deli on Seventh Avenue at 55th Street "makes a hell of a pastrami sandwich." And Junior's in downtown Brooklyn at Flatbush and DeKalb serves what a lot of people think is the best cheese cake in the city. I've certainly never had better.

Whew—New York! Say what you want about it but for restaurants, no other city can compare. And I haven't even talked about Brazilian restaurants, or Lebanese, or Greek, or Cuban-Chinese...

To evaluate a new Jewish restaurant, use the Naiman test: order chopped liver, cold borsht with sour cream and noodle kugel or rice pudding for dessert (or as many of those items as they have). It's rare to find a restaurant that makes any of them well. But if you find one that does, even if everything else they make stinks, you can just keep ordering that same meal.